Standards-Based Connections
Reading
Grade 3

Carson-Dellosa Publishing, LLC
Greensboro, North Carolina

Credits
Content Editor: Amy Payne
Copy Editor: Christine M. Schwab

Visit *carsondellosa.com* for correlations to Common Core, state, national, and Canadian provincial standards.

Carson-Dellosa Publishing, LLC
PO Box 35665
Greensboro, NC 27425 USA
carsondellosa.com

ISBN 978-1-4838-2476-5

01-188151151

Table of Contents

Introduction

Reading comprehension is an essential skill for enabling school, college, and career success. This book focuses on five reading comprehension skills: story elements, summarizing, compare and contrast, cause and effect, and inferring. Emphasized are the reading standards in the Common Core State Standards.

The reading standards set expectations for each grade level and define what students should understand and be able to do. They are designed to be more rigorous and allow for students to justify their thinking. They reflect the knowledge that is necessary for success in college and career readiness. Students who master the standards as they advance through the grades will exhibit the following capabilities:

1. They demonstrate independence.
2. They build strong content knowledge.
3. They respond to the varying demands of audience, task, purpose, and discipline.
4. They comprehend as well as critique.
5. They value evidence.
6. They use technology and digital media strategically and capably.
7. They come to understand other perspectives and cultures.*

How to Use This Book

This book is a collection of grade-appropriate practice pages aligned to the reading sections of the Common Core State Standards for English Language Arts. Included is a skill matrix to show exactly which standards are addressed on the practice pages. Also included are a skill assessment and a skill assessment analysis. Use the assessment at the beginning of the year or at any time you wish to assess your students' mastery of certain standards. The analysis connects each test item to a practice page or set of practice pages so that you can review skills with students who struggle in certain areas.

Common Core State Standards Alignment Matrix

Page #	12	13	14	15	16	17	18	19	20	21	22	23	24	25	26	27	28	29	30	31	32	33	34	35	36	37	38	39	40	41	42	43	44	45	46	47	48	49	50	51
3.RL.1	•					•		•		•		•		•		•	•		•		•					•		•		•								•		•
3.RL.2						•								•		•				•								•		•		•								
3.RL.3	•			•		•				•				•			•					•		•		•												•		•
3.RL.4	•																							•											•					
3.RL.5						•																		•											•					
3.RL.6				•																						•		•												
3.RL.7																										•														•
3.RL.9									•								•																				•			•
3.RL.10			•		•		•		•		•		•		•				•			•		•			•			•		•						•		•
3.RI.1		•																																						
3.RI.2																		•																•		•				
3.RI.3																		•																		•				
3.RI.4																																		•						
3.RI.5																													•											
3.RI.6																																		•						
3.RI.7																																								
3.RI.8		•																																		•				
3.RI.9																																								
3.RI.10		•																															•		•					

Page #	52	53	54	55	56	57	58	59	60	61	62	63	64	65	66	67	68	69	70	71	72	73	74	75	76	77	78	79	80	81	82	83	84	85	86	87	88	89	90	91
3.RL.1													•			•			•	•							•		•							•		•		
3.RL.2													•																											•
3.RL.3													•						•	•												•				•		•		
3.RL.4																											•					•		•				•		
3.RL.5															•																					•				•
3.RL.6							•								•	•																								•
3.RL.7																							•	•																
3.RL.9							•																							•				•						
3.RL.10					•					•			•			•				•							•	•	•		•		•		•		•		•	
3.RI.1				•		•		•									•					•																		
3.RI.2																					•		•																	
3.RI.3		•		•													•				•	•			•	•														
3.RI.4		•				•															•																			
3.RI.5		•		•		•		•		•																														
3.RI.6																	•											•												
3.RI.7					•			•		•														•																
3.RI.8										•																														
3.RI.9			•		•																		•																	
3.RI.10	•		•		•		•		•																		•		•											

© Carson-Dellosa • CD-104660

Wild Weather in Wilton

Read the article. Study the chart. Answer the questions.

WILTON, WA The people in Wilton have seen some wild weather. Meteorologists are baffled.

It all started last Sunday. At 12:36 am, the heat quickly rose 20 degrees to a balmy 58°F. A temperature of 42°F is normal for January weather here in Wilton. Many locals enjoyed the warm weather. They went for walks and had picnics.

At 12:36 pm, the readings dropped to 26°F. Snow started to fall minutes later. Five feet of snow had settled on the ground by 2:00 pm.

Five EF4 twisters formed out in the country at 11:36 pm. They spun through the county. Snow was thrown miles into the air. Then, the funnels spun out. There was no snow left on the ground.

This same pattern of weather has happened each day since then. All local meteorologists are working together to figure out what is going on. They want to try to find a way to stop this wild weather. The Wilton Press will post daily updates.

The Enhanced Fujita Tornado Scale	
EF Number	**Wind Gusts (mph)**
0	65–85
1	86–110
2	111–135
3	136–165
4	166–200
5	Over 200

1. What is causing this weather event to happen in Wilton, WA? _____

2. Why did the author include the tornado scale? _____

3. What is a meteorologist? _____

   What information in the text helped you find your answer?_____

4. What is the main idea of this article?_____

5. What information does the author use to support the main idea?_____

   _____

6. What does the word *locals* mean in this text?

   a. a place nearby   b. people who live nearby

   c. locations   d. all of the above

7. How is the text organized?

   a. comparing and contrasting   b. cause and effect   c. sequential order

Twisting, Turning

Read the poem. Answer the questions.

Twist and turn

around and round

look out if it touches the ground!

clouds of dust

Dirt

and Debris

Take cover!

But not underneath

that tree!

Find a place safe underground

Until that train stops making sound!

Once the dust has finally settled

Broken twigs

and

twisted metal.

But all are safe

in this sleepy town

after this tornado touched down.

8. What genre of text is this? _____

9. Complete the plot line using the events in the text.

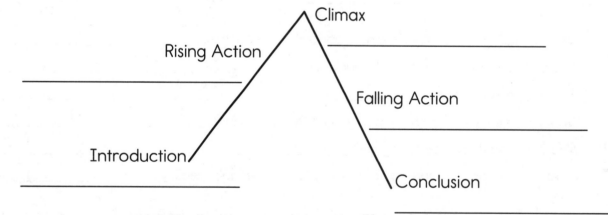

10. How did the author use the placement of the text to create an image in the reader's mind?

_____

11. What type of figurative language is used in line 11? _____

What does the author mean? _____

12. Write a new title for this text. Explain why it would be a good title. _____

_____

Use the texts on pages 5 and 6 to complete the activity.

13. Write a comparison essay telling how the two texts are alike and different. Be sure your essay includes

- an introduction of the topic;

- facts and details relating to the topic;

- words and phrases that link ideas (such as *another, for example, also, because*);

- precise language;

- a conclusion related to the topic.

Write the first draft of your essay below. Read your essay to another person to see if there are any suggestions. Then, rewrite your final draft on another sheet of paper or on the computer.

_____

_____

_____

_____

_____

_____

_____

_____

_____

_____

_____

_____

_____

_____

_____

_____

_____

The following are letters that Terry received from two friends who had gone away over spring vacation. Read the two letters. Answer the questions that follow.

Pen Pals

Dear Terry,

Hi from New York City. So far I have been to two museums. The Metropolitan Museum of Art was great. The American Museum of Natural History took all day. The art museum had over two million works of art! We saw dinosaur bones at the natural history museum. We also took a tour of the NBC studios at Rockefeller Center. For lunch, we went to Central Park. Monday we are going to take the ferry to see the Statue of Liberty. Then, we visit the Empire State Building.

Charles

Dear Terry,

We are having a great time in Los Angeles! Yesterday, we went to the Natural History Museum. We saw bones from prehistoric animals. It was so cool! We've also been to Griffith Park. There, we visited a butterfly garden. Yesterday, we took a tour of the NBC studios. Tuesday, we are going to Anaheim. That is where Disneyland is! I can't wait! See you in a few days.

Your Buddy,
Aaron

14.	Which city has the Empire State Building? _____

15.	Which city has a butterfly garden inside a park? _____

16.	Which friend saw dinosaur bones in a museum? _____

17.	Which friend visited a museum with many paintings? _____

18.	What tour were both friends able to take on their different trips? _____

_____

19.	In what city is Disneyland? _____

20.	In what city is Central Park? _____

Read the passage. Answer the questions.

It's All in the Past

There are many history museums. Two of the largest are on opposite sides of the country from each other.

The Natural History Museum in Los Angeles, CA, is over 100 years old. The museum has had history, art, and science collections for people to see since 1913. Today, the building has many exhibits.[1] It has birds, mammals, dinosaurs, gems, and minerals. It also houses a Discovery Center for kids to explore.

The American Museum of Natural History is in New York, NY. It opened its doors in 1869. It has had many exhibits as well. At the AMNH, you can see birds, reptiles, mammals, gems, minerals, and early people. The museum also has many displays about planets and space. It has a children's Discovery Room.

These buildings are truly history-filled, fun places to visit!

The Natural History Museum and the American Museum of Natural History are on opposite sides of the country from each other.

[1] exhibit: an object or group of objects put out for people to see

21. How are the two museums alike? _____

_____

How are the two museums are different?_____

_____

22. What is the small number next to the word *exhibits* in paragraph 2? _____

What does this tell you? _____

23. What opinion does the author have about the museums? _____

Do you agree?_____

Use the texts on pages 8 and 9 to answer the questions and complete the activity.

24. What is the difference between the texts on pages 8 and 9? _____

_____

25. Why did the author include the map on page 9? _____

_____

26. What text feature could have been included on page 8 to help readers? _____

_____

How would this text feature have helped the readers? _____

_____

27. Draw the text feature below:

After you score each student's skill assessment pages, match any incorrectly answered problems to the table below. Use the corresponding practice pages for any problem areas, and ensure that each student receives remediation in these areas.

Answer Key: 1. No one knows. 2. to let us know how strong the tornados were; 3. someone who studies weather; wild weather, meteorologists are baffled; 4. Wilton has had some wild weather lately. 5. The heat rose, the temperature dropped, it snowed, and there were tornados. 6. b; 7. c; 8. poetry;

9. 10. The author made the poem look like a tornado. 11. metaphor; The author compares the tornado to a train. 12. Answers will vary. 13. Answers will vary. 14. New York City; 15. Los Angeles; 16. both Charles and Aaron; 17. Charles; 18. NBC studios tour; 19. Anaheim; 20. New York City; 21. They have some of the same exhibits. AMNH has an early people exhibit. 22. a footnote, It tells you the definition of the word. 23. The museums are fun. Answers will vary. 24. Page 8 is fiction and page 9 is nonfiction. 25. to show where the two museums are located; 26. Answers will vary but may include a map, captions, or photos. 27. Answers will vary.

Comprehension Skill	Common Core State Standards*	Assessment Item(s)	Practice Page(s)
Reading Standards for Literature			
Story Elements	3.RL.1, 3.RL.3, 3.RL.4, 3.RL.7, 3.RL.10	7, 8, 11, 19, 20	12, 14, 16–28, 30–34, 36–43, 48–51, 62, 64, 65, 67, 69, 70, 71, 78–80, 82–90
Summarizing	3.RL.2	4, 5, 9, 12, 13	17, 25, 27, 31, 41, 43, 64, 91
Compare and Contrast	3.RL.6, 3.RL.9	13–18	15, 28, 39, 41, 48, 66, 67, 81, 85, 89, 91
Cause and Effect	3.RL.3, 3.RL.5	1, 13	13, 15, 17, 21, 25, 28, 33, 35, 37, 43, 49, 51, 64, 66, 70, 71, 83, 87, 89, 91
Inferring	3.RL.1, 3.RL.4	11	12, 33, 43, 78, 83, 85, 89
Reading Standards for Informational Text			
Story Elements	3.RI.1, 3.RI.4, 3.RI.5, 3.RI.7, 3.RI.10	2, 3, 6, 22, 25, 27	13, 44–46, 52–61, 68, 73, 75–77
Summarizing	3.RI.2	23	29, 45, 47, 72, 74
Compare and Contrast	3.RI.6, 3.RI.8, 3.RI.9	21, 24	13, 45, 47, 55, 57, 61, 63, 74, 77
Cause and Effect	3.RI.3, 3.RI.5, 3.RI.8	26	13, 29, 41, 47, 53, 55, 57, 59, 61, 63, 68, 72, 73, 76, 77
Inferring	3.RI.4	10, 24	45, 53, 57, 72

* © Copyright 2010. National Governors Association Center for Best Practices and Council of Chief State School Officers. All rights reserved.

Name_____

The Fox and the Grapes

Read the story. Answer the questions.

On a hot summer's day, a red fox went for a walk. He soon became very thirsty under the scorching sun. He looked for a pond, or a brook, or even a puddle from which to drink, but he had no luck. Then he spied a fat bunch of juicy grapes. They were ripening on a vine that was hanging over a high branch. "Just the thing to quench my thirst," Fox thought.

Fox took a running jump at the grapes, but he missed. He stepped back a few paces. He eyed the grapes greedily, gathered his strength, and leaped for the grapes. His nose brushed the grapes and smelled their sweet scent, but he could not reach them. Fox tried again and again. He jumped and jumped until he could jump no more. Finally, he gathered what energy he had left and tried to climb the tree. He slid down the trunk and landed in a sad heap on the ground.

After a few moment's rest, Fox mustered his dignity and trotted down the path. He declared to himself and any who could hear him, "I am sure those grapes are sour anyway."

1. What was the fox's problem?

   a. He was thirsty.   b. He was hungry.   c. He was lonely.

2. What did the fox find to solve his problem?

   a. a pond   b. a puddle   c. a fat bunch of juicy grapes

3. In the third paragraph, what is the meaning of the word *mustered*?

   a. gathered   b. yelled   c. ate

4. List two character traits that describe the fox in this story. _____

   _____

5. "The Fox and the Grapes" is a fable by Aesop. The moral of the tale is "It is easy to reject what you cannot have." What does this mean? _____

   _____

   _____

   _____

☐ I can ask and answer questions about a text I have read.
☐ I can look back at the text to find answers.
☐ I can describe characters in a story.
☐ I can figure out the meaning of words and phrases in a story.

Laura Ingalls Wilder

Read the information about Laura Ingalls Wilder. In the activity, write **P** before the sentence if it tells about a problem in Laura's family history. Write **S** if the sentence tells about a solution to a problem.

Laura Ingalls Wilder wrote eight books about her childhood. She grew up in Wisconsin, Kansas, Minnesota, and South Dakota in the 1800s. During her life, she and her family faced many problems.

The Ingalls family lost their farm in Kansas. By mistake, they had built it on land that belonged to an Osage tribe. The family had worked hard to build a house and barn. But they had to leave it and find somewhere else to live.

Several years later, the Ingalls family moved to Minnesota. They lived in a dugout while they built another farm. During this time, Laura's sister Mary became sick. Her eyes were damaged, and she became blind. Laura and her family worked hard to raise money for Mary. When they finally had enough, they sent Mary to a school for blind students. There, she learned how to read braille. She also learned other skills to help her have a better life.

Later, Laura's family moved to South Dakota. They claimed land both in town and out on the prairie. Laura and her sisters liked their new home and neighbors. But, life on the prairie could be dangerous.

One winter, the trains could not get through the snow to deliver food. Everyone in town almost starved to death. Laura's future husband, Almanzo, risked his life to help. He traveled to a distant farm to get wheat. The townspeople used the wheat to make bread. It was their only food for the rest of the winter. When spring came, the trains finally arrived and the town was saved.

_____ 1. The family sent Mary to a school for blind people.

_____ 2. Trains could not reach Laura's town one snowy winter.

_____ 3. The Ingalls family settled on land that actually belonged to the Osage tribe.

_____ 4. Almanzo risked his life to help get wheat from a farm.

_____ 5. Mary Ingalls went blind after she became ill.

_____ 6. In the spring, the trains arrived with supplies for the town.

☐ **I can look back at the text to find my answers.**
☐ **I can use sentences and paragraphs to figure out the text structure.**
☐ **I can read and comprehend grade-level informational texts.**

Name_____

A Day on the Trail

Read the two versions of the story. Then, answer the questions on page 15.

Dylan's story:

Today was the day I had been waiting for—our class nature hike! I was so excited, I got up at five o'clock in the morning. I was the first person on the bus. On the way to the trail, Mr. Evans told us about the different animals, rocks, and plants that we would be looking for, and he gave us each a list to fill out. The person who found the most items on the list would get a prize. It was an excellent, hand-held microscope for fieldwork! Of course, I was determined to win.

A lot of the kids did not understand that they needed to be quiet to see any wildlife. I stayed behind the group and moved very slowly down the trail. A snake slithered right in front of me, and a little red squirrel nearly ran across my foot! I saw a baby rabbit that was eating a leaf bigger than he was. I also saw a robin, two mourning doves, and a blue jay. I found 16 different leaf specimens and did scratch tests on five different rocks.

I was sorry when we had to leave, but I was thrilled to win the field microscope!

Danny's story:

Today was the day I had been dreading—our class nature hike. My mother could barely drag me out of bed. I hate being outdoors; its so much more interesting playing computer games. Plus, I always get poison ivy, even if I am miles from the plants!

On the bus, Mr. Evans handed out lists we were supposed to fill in . . . as if the hike itself wasn't bad enough! I lost my canteen right away; it rolled down a cliff and bounced into the river. Then I ripped my T-shirt on a bush with huge, monster-sized thorns. I did manage to find a couple of rocks, but only because I tripped on them. I am sure there was not a single animal anywhere on the trail. I did not see one. Of course, I did fall down a lot, so maybe I scared them off.

By the time we got back to the bus, I was hot, dirty, and tired. I was so glad to get back to civilization, I nearly hugged my computer. But by bedtime, it was clear that somehow, I had gotten poison ivy again. I was covered with it!

☐   I can read and comprehend grade-level fiction texts.

Name_____

A Day on the Trail (cont.)

Answer the questions about the stories on page 14.

Write the name of the character described by each phrase:

1. Thrilled to win the microscope _____

2. Disgusted to find he had poison ivy _____

3. Filled in the whole list _____

4. Found five rocks _____

5. Fell down _____

6. Got up early _____

7. Got up late _____

8. Saw no animals or birds _____

9. Saw a reptile, two mammals, and four birds _____

10. Ended the trip tired and dirty _____

11. Ended the trip excited and happy _____

12. Circle the words that describe Dylan's day.

    exciting   boring   interesting   good

    difficult   happy   bad   tiring

13. Circle the words that describe Danny's day.

    scary   itchy   enjoyable   good

    difficult   happy   bad   tiring

14. The setting in this story was the same for both, but the two characters reacted very differently to it. Which character's reaction was most like yours would be? _____

    Why? _____

    _____

    _____

☐ **I can describe characters in a story.**
☐ **I can explain how characters' actions affect the story.**
☐ **I can compare my point of view to that of the narrator or characters.**

Woodie Lost and Found

Read the story. Answer questions about it on page 17.

Woodie was scared. For the second time in her young life, she was lost. When the branch fell on her little house and fence, she had just barely escaped. She scrambled across her pen as quick as lightning. The thunder crashed, and Woodie leaped across the fallen fence into the woods. Now the rain poured down. The wind howled. The little woodchuck shivered under a big oak tree. She did not know what to do.

When Woodie was a baby, she had gotten lost in the woods. She could not find food for herself. She hurt her paw, and she spent hours licking it to make it feel better. All day, she scratched at a small hole in the ground to try to make a burrow. This made her even more hungry.

But then one day, Rita had found her. Rita had knelt down by Woodie's badly made burrow and held out an apple. Slowly, Woodie limped out and took the apple. It was the best thing she had ever tasted in her life. Rita took the baby woodchuck to the wildlife center where Woodie had lived ever since. Most of the animals at the wildlife center were orphans. Rita taught them how to live in the wild and then let them go when they were ready. But, Woodie's paw did not heal well, and Rita knew Woodie would never able to live in the wild like other woodchucks. So Rita made Woodie a small house at the wildlife center. Woodie even had a job; she visited schools with Rita so that students could learn all about woodchucks.

But now the storm had ruined Woodie's house. Scared by the loud crash, Woodie had run so fast that she had gone into the woods by mistake. Woodie did not know how to find her way back home again. Where was Rita?

At dawn, the rain ended. Woodie came to a big stream. She drank some water. She sniffed the air. Maybe the center was across the stream. Woodie jumped onto a rock and then hopped to another one. She landed on her bad paw and fell into the fast-moving water. She struggled to keep her nose above water. The current tossed her against a tangle of broken branches from the storm. Woodie clung to the branches with all her might.

"There she is!" Woodie heard Rita's voice. She saw Rita with Ben, another worker from the center. Rita waded over to the branches. In moments, Woodie was safe in Rita's arms. Rita wrapped a blanket around the tired, soaking-wet woodchuck. Woodie purred her thanks. By the time Ben pulled the van into the parking lot at the wildlife center, Woodie was fast asleep.

☐ **I can read and comprehend grade-level fiction texts.**

Woodie Lost and Found (cont.)

Circle the answer for each question about the story on page 16.

1. What was the problem in the story "Woodie Lost and Found"?
    a. Woodie hurt her paw.
    b. Woodie had been lost as a baby.
    c. Woodie got lost during a big storm.

2. Who is the main character in the story?
    a. Rita, the wildlife expert
    b. Woodie, a woodchuck
    c. Ben, a wildlife center worker

3. What happens right before Woodie gets lost in the storm?
    a. She is unable to dig a burrow for herself.
    b. Rita loses Woodie on a trip to a school.
    c. The fence of Woodie's pen falls down in the storm.

4. Why do you think we are told about Woodie's life as a baby?
    a. so we know that Woodie has been lost before—she knows what to do
    b. so we know that Woodie cannot live in the wild—she is in danger
    c. so we know Woodie trusts people—she knows if she waits, someone will always come to find her

5. What is the climax of the story?
    a. A branch falls on Woodie's house and she barely gets out in time.
    b. Woodie shivers under a big oak, all alone in the storm.
    c. Woodie falls into the water as she tries to cross a stream.

6. What is the solution, or resolution, of the story?
    a. Rita finds Woodie under the tree and gives her an apple.
    b. Rita finds Woodie, rescues her from the stream, and takes her home.
    c. Rita finds Woodie and takes her on a visit to a school.

7. Circle the words or phrases that best describe Woody.

    tough   determined   scared   gives up easily

8. Circle the words or phrases that best describe Rita.

    thoughtless   caring   determined   gives up easily

☐ I can ask and answer questions about a text I have read.
☐ I can retell stories using details and use them to understand the main idea.
☐ I can use proper terms to name parts of text.
☐ I can describe characters in a story.

Jorge's Tadpoles

Read the story. Answer questions about it on page 19.

Jorge sat cross-legged on the dusty window seat. He stared at the foggy woods. How he wished he was back in New Mexico! At that moment, he would probably be playing air hockey with his friends, Carlos and Dustin.

Jorge's family had moved to California at the beginning of the year. He had not made even one new friend in two whole months. His sadness felt selfish. Everyone else in his family was so happy in their new home.

Jorge's sister, Anita, had found a kitten in the woods outside their home. His mother had let her keep it. His father has a great new job at the local television station. He loves telling the family about all of the celebrities he meets. His mother likes to go running on the nearby beach every morning. She was also taking classes at the community college in the afternoons. Everyone was having a great time—everyone except for Jorge, that is.

Jorge did not know what to do. None of the boys in his class lived nearby. Besides, they all had known each other since kindergarten. Jorge was an outsider. The boys were polite enough. They could even be friendly. But, after they said hello in the morning, they wandered off into groups. He was never included. Jorge could not blame them. He and his old friends had done the same thing lots of times.

Jorge decided to stop feeling so sad. Friends or no friends, it was a perfectly good Saturday afternoon. He opened the back door and stepped outside. The tall trees smelled spicy in the sea air. Jorge began to feel better. He took the back stairs two at a time. He hurried down the familiar path into the woods. A carpet of fallen leaves cushioned his step.

Jorge was surprised when he reached the creek. Something had changed. Water no longer tumbled over the rocks. There were only small pools where the creek should be. He looked carefully into the pools of water. He could see they were filled with tiny, dark creatures. They were packed closely together. They could hardly move through the small amount of water.

Jorge could tell right away that the creatures were tadpoles. He had studied them in science class last year. A few of them had grown back legs. But, they were not yet ready to live on land.

The remaining water was drying up fast. Suddenly, Jorge understood why everyone on the news was talking about a drought. Hardly any rain had fallen in the past month. The water in town was getting very low.

Jorge could not make it rain. But he could help some of the tadpoles. He hurried back to his house to get a glass jar. When he returned, he scooped up some of the tadpoles with the water. As he held up the jar, he could see them swimming around inside.

☐　**I can read and comprehend grade-level fiction texts.**

Jorge's Tadpoles (cont.)

Jorge decided to take the tadpoles to school on Monday morning. He was sure that his science teacher, Mrs. Abdul, would know how to help them. The other students were excited to see the tadpoles. They gathered around to study them in the jar.

Mrs. Abdul came up with a plan to help the tadpoles. She found a tank to raise them in. She asked Jorge to help her fill it with water. Then, the class put together a schedule to feed the tadpoles and care for them. Everyone would take turns helping out, and Jorge would organize everything.

All of the students enjoyed taking care of Jorge's tadpoles. They learned a lot about frogs and how they grow. They also learned a lot about Jorge and his life back in New Mexico. By the time the last tadpole turned into a frog, Jorge had a lot of new friends.

Circle the answer for each question about the story you just read.

1. Who is the main character in the story?

   a. Jorge

   b. Dustin

   c. Mrs. Abdul

2. What does the main character want?

   a. to learn about tadpoles

   b. to find a kitten

   c. to make friends

3. Where does the story take place?

   a. in California

   b. in New Mexico

   c. in the South

4. When does the story take place?

   a. a long time ago

   b. in the future

   c. now

5. What happens at the end of the story?

   a. Jorge finds tadpoles in the woods.

   b. Jorge's class helps raise the tadpoles.

   c. Jorge learns that tadpoles grow into frogs.

□ I can ask and answer questions about a text I have read.
□ I can look back at a text to find answers.

Javier's Bike

Read the story. Answer the questions about it on page 21.

Every boy on Javier's block had a bike, and Javier wanted one too. He often watched his friends ride down to the park. They waved to him as they went by. "Come on, Javier," they called. He just waved back. It was eight long blocks to the park. Walking was very slow, and by the time he got there, it was time to turn around and go back home.

One night, Javier was helping his mother wash dishes. "Please, can I have a bike?" he asked.

His mother shook her head as she handed him a plate to dry. "I'm sorry, Javier. A bike costs a lot of money, and now is not a good time. Your sister needs new shoes, and your grandfather in Mexico is sick. We have to send him money for a doctor. Maybe next year we can buy you a bike."

Javier sighed and finished helping her, then went to his room. He did not want his mother to see how sad he was. He sat down on his bed and stared at the wall. How would he ever get a bike?

Suddenly, he remembered a saying he had heard in class. "Where there is a will, there is a way." It meant that you could get what you wanted. You just had to want it enough and keep trying until you found a way.

The next day was Saturday. Javier was about to walk to the park when he saw Mrs. Martinez next door. She was pulling weeds in her garden. There were too many weeds for her to pull by herself. Her sons had grown up and moved away to other towns, and her husband was away on business. There was no else there who could help her.

Javier said he would help. She smiled and told him to get a pair of gloves, pointing to a shed behind the house. When he opened the door, he saw the gloves. He also saw a bike. It was old and the tires were flat, but it looked beautiful to Javier.

He heard a voice behind him. "That was my youngest son's bike," Mrs. Martinez said. "Do you like it?"

"Oh yes!" replied Javier. He wished that it could be his bike.

"Get the gloves and help me and when we finish, I will give you a cool drink," she said.

Javier picked up the gloves slowly. He turned around to find Mrs. Martinez smiling at him. "And I'll give you the bike too, of course. After all, we can't have you walking to the park every day."

How could he have dreamed that she would give him such a fine gift for such a little favor? Javier grinned from ear to ear. At last, he would have a bike of his own!

☐   **I can read and comprehend grade-level fiction texts.**

Javier's Bike (cont.)

Answer the questions about the story on page 20.

1. What did Javier want?

   _____

2. Why was he unable to get what he wanted?

   _____

   _____

3. One Saturday, Javier offered to help someone. Who did he help and why?

   _____

   _____

4. How did Javier get what he wanted?

   _____

   _____

5. Based on the stories on pages 18 and 20, how are "Jorge's Tadpoles" and "Javier's Bike" similar?

   _____

   _____

6. Based on the stories on pages 18 and 20, how are "Jorge's Tadpoles" and "Javier's Bike" different?

   _____

   _____

☐ I can look back at the text to find answers.
☐ I can describe characters in a story.
☐ I can compare and contrast themes, settings, and plots of stories that have something in common, such as the same author.

The Case of the Missing Heirloom

Read the story. Answer the questions about it on page 23.

Demitri waited on the playground in the shade of a big tree. If the other members of the Mystery Society did not arrive soon, he would have to meet the new client alone. Then, he saw Jimmy and Sabena running across the yard. Jimmy reached him first. "Sorry," he gasped. "We just got back from a field trip."

"OK, well, we should get started," Demitri said. "I got an email this morning from a new boy in the neighborhood. He is in my little brother's class. He has a problem and needs our help."

"Great!" said Sabena. "We haven't had a case all month."

"Actually, we haven't had a case since last year," Jimmy replied.

Sabena shrugged. "So, who's keeping track?"

The group walked to a house in the next block. Demitri pulled out a piece of paper. He checked an address that was written on it. "This is it," he told them. The other two kids followed him up the path to the door.

At the front door, Demitri rang the bell. There was no answer at first. So, he rang the bell again. After a moment, the big door opened. A small boy in a red-striped T-shirt and a pair of jeans stood on the other side. "Are you the Mystery Society?" he asked.

"That's us," Demitri replied. "I'm Demitri, and these are my associates, Jimmy and Sabena. May we come in?"

"Sure," said the boy. "I guess your brother Jack told you about me. I'm Andre, but everybody calls me Dre." He led them to a small TV room and closed the door.

"What is the problem, Dre?" Demitri asked.

"I . . . I lost my grandfather's watch," Dre replied. He looked as though he were about to cry. "If my mom finds out, I don't know what she'll do. That watch was worth a lot of money."

"It's OK, Dre," Sabena said gently. "We'll help you find it."

"When did you see it last?" Jimmy asked.

"I saw it the day after we moved," Dre said. "It was in the top drawer of my dresser. When I looked for it yesterday, it was gone."

Dre took them upstairs to his room. He pointed to the dresser. Demitri and Jimmy asked Dre more questions. They wanted to know how big the watch was and what it looked like. As Dre described it, Sabena took the top drawer all the way out of the dresser. She reached into the space where the drawer had been. Excitedly, she pulled out the watch. The Mystery Society had cracked another case!

___

I can read and comprehend grade-level fiction texts.

The Case of the Missing Heirloom (cont.)

Fill in the circle in front of each correct answer about the story on page 22.

1. How did Dre hear about the Mystery Society?

   ◯ from Demitri's brother

   ◯ from Sabena

   ◯ from the school newspaper

2. What had Dre lost?

   ◯ a pen

   ◯ a watch

   ◯ 10 dollars

3. How did Dre contact the Mystery Society?

   ◯ by email

   ◯ by telephone

   ◯ through the mail

4. Why were Jimmy and Sabena so late?

   ◯ Their teacher made them stay after class.

   ◯ They had just come from a field trip.

   ◯ They had lost track of time.

5. Why did Dre close the door to the TV room?

   ◯ He did not want anyone to leave.

   ◯ He wanted to watch TV.

   ◯ He did not want his mother to hear.

6. Who solved the mystery?

   ◯ Demitri

   ◯ Sabena

   ◯ Jimmy

☐ I can ask and answer questions about a text I have read.
☐ I can look back at the text to find answers.

Bitsy's Bad Summer

Read the story. Fill in the web on page 25.

Bitsy was a gray squirrel who lived in an oak tree behind a yellow house. Her home was a nice, dry nest built of twigs. Bitsy lined the nest with soft fur and feathers. Each day, she gathered nuts and bark for her supper. Bitsy hid tasty acorns so she would have food in the winter. When she could, Bitsy dined upon mushrooms, grasses, and seeds. Sometimes, she scurried up the neighbor's bird feeder for a snack. Bitsy drank from the little stream that meandered through the woods, or she lapped dew on leaves and grass. Bitsy enjoyed her quiet life.

One summer day, a tall woman moved into the yellow house. She carried a fat, black cat with leaf-green eyes. Bitsy knew a few cats. A multicolored cat lived in the house next door. That cat stayed inside and watched birds from the windowsill. An orange tabby cat sometimes wandered into Bitsy's yard to lounge in the sun-dappled grass. Once, Bitsy ran right up to the orange cat's nose. The cat reached a lazy paw towards Bitsy, but she was too slow to scare Bitsy. The black cat was different.

Every morning, the tall woman opened the door. The cat she called Midnight stalked outside and crouched beneath the oak tree. She stared at Bitsy with her leaf-green eyes. Bitsy flicked her tail and scolded the cat. Midnight coiled, ready to spring, her black tail swishing back and forth. Bitsy sensed danger. Late in the evening, the woman opened the door for Midnight. By the time the cat was safely inside, it was time for Bitsy to snuggle up in her nest, safe from predators that hunt in the dark.

Midnight kept Bitsy from burying acorns and dining on seeds and mushrooms on the ground. Once, Bitsy raced down her tree to bury an acorn before the cat saw her. The tip of a sharp claw raked Bitsy's tail as she raced back up the tree. "Too close!" she thought. "I must be clever, or I will starve!"

Early the next morning, Bitsy scurried down the tree to search for food before Midnight returned. When the door opened, and Midnight took up her post beneath the oak, Bitsy jumped from branch to branch, climbing along fences and rooftops in search of safe places to eat and drink. She was constantly alert to dangers from wild animals and pets. She sniffed the air for dogs and cats. She kept her ears and eyes open for foxes, raccoons, and hawks. It was hard work, but she did not starve.

One day, when the leaves were changing colors, the tall woman packed her bags and her cat in the car and drove away. Bitsy raced up and down her tree in celebration. Her bad summer was over at last!

☐ **I can read and comprehend grade-level fiction texts.**

Bitsy's Bad Summer (cont.)

Fill in the web with information from the story on page 24.

Bitsy's food

Bitsy's tree

Bitsy's Life

The new guest

Bitsy's home

Bitsy's Problem

The new guest's pet

The new pet's habit

Bitsy might starve because _____.

Bitsy was scared because _____.

Bitsy had to be careful of

Bitsy's Solution

How Bitsy handled the problem

Time of year the problem stopped

☐ I can look back at the text to find answers.
☐ I can retell stories using details and use them to understand the main idea.
☐ I can describe characters in a story.
☐ I can explain how characters' actions affect the story.

A Mystery in the Night

Read the story. Answer the questions about it on page 27.

On a rainy night in October 1857, Joshua finally found the answer to the mystery. So many times, he had asked his mother about doors closing and steps creaking in the night. She had said, "You must have been dreaming, son." So many times, he had asked his father about the sound of horses in the night. He had said, "It must have been closer to morning than you thought, Josh." But on this night, Joshua knew he was not dreaming and was not wrong about the time.

When he heard the kitchen door close, he got out of bed. He walked slowly down the stairs. In the hall, he saw the dim light of a single candle. Then, he was face to face with his father. Behind his father stood three people: a man, a woman, and a child. They looked tired and scared, and there were leaves clinging to their clothes. Their skin was dark and their eyes were wide at the sight of Joshua.

"Son, go to your room," said Joshua's father in a stern voice. Joshua backed down the hall, still looking. Later, Joshua's mother came into his room. "We were wrong to lie to you," she said softly. "You are old enough to know the truth. Your father and I are running a station on the Underground Railroad."

Joshua caught his breath. He had heard about this at school. Some people who felt that slavery was wrong were helping slaves to escape. The slaves made their way from place to place. At each "station" they were given food, water, and help to the next friendly place.

"That family is eating supper now," said his mother. "Tomorrow night, after they rest, your father will drive them to Smith's Landing. Someone will meet them there."

Joshua nodded. His mother looked at him and said, "Do you understand, Joshua? Do you know that you must never say a word about this to anyone?"

Joshua understood. He knew that his father could be put in jail for helping slaves to escape because it was against the law. He would not tell anyone, not even his best friend, James. Joshua and James had talked about the Underground Railroad. They had wondered if anyone they knew was working with the secret organization. Joshua longed to tell James his secret, but he knew he had to keep his promise. His father and mother were doing a good thing and protecting other people. Now, he had to protect his parents and keep his family safe.

When he became an adult, Joshua learned more about the help his parents had given. He was proud of their part in the Underground Railroad. They had risked their own freedom and possibly lives to protect this secret group of paths and safe houses. The slaves they helped traveled secretly from place to place until they reached freedom. The houses where they stayed were called stations. Guides, like Joshua's parents, were known as conductors. Thousands of slaves traveled the Underground Railroad to freedom in the 1800s.

☐ **I can read and comprehend grade-level fiction texts.**

A Mystery in the Night (cont.)

Write **first**, **second**, **third**, **fourth**, or **fifth** to show the correct order of the events in the story on page 26.

_____ 1. Joshua decides not to tell James about his parents and their work to help escaped slaves.

_____ 2. Joshua goes down the stairs and into the back hallway.

_____ 3. Joshua sees his father with a family of escaped slaves.

_____ 4. Joshua is told that the noises he hears at night are just his imagination.

_____ 5. Joshua's mother tells him that their house is a station on the Underground Railroad.

"A Mystery in the Night" is only part of a story. Write **before** or **after** next to each event to show when it would take place in relation to the part of the story you have read.

_____ 6. Joshua and James hear about a secret organization called "The Underground Railroad" from some of their classmates.

_____ 7. Joshua's father drives the slave family to Smith's Landing.

_____ 8. Joshua wonders if he really dreamed the strange sound of voices coming from the kitchen one night.

_____ 9. James and Joshua go fishing and wonder if anyone they know is helping slaves to escape from the South.

_____ 10. Joshua's mother mends some old clothes but will not tell Joshua why she is fixing the clothing.

☐ I can look back at the text to find answers.
☐ I can retell stories using details.

Name_____

Two Friends, Two Vacations

Read the two letters. Fill in the chart to contrast the two characters' problems.

Dear Dennis,

Well, here I am at my aunt's house. How am I ever going to get everything she wants done? I only got to sit down for five minutes before she had me painting the stairs. She wants me to wash the walls in the kitchen. She wants me to wax the floor in the hallway. And, did I tell you about the barn? She wants me to clean out all of the old hay in the barn! It's got to be 100-year-old hay! Every night I fall into bed, and then it feels like I get two minutes of sleep before it's morning again. I sure hope I survive and see you at school in September!

Ralph

Dear Dennis,

Hey, I miss you! It is so quiet here at my grandmother's house. She doesn't own a TV! She must be the last person on the planet without one. All morning long, we sit and read. Then we eat lunch, and then we go for a little walk. After that, we read some more. The only time I get to see anyone is when we shop for groceries. Plus, Grandma won't let me help her with anything. If I offer to wash the dishes, she says, "No, dear, you are on vacation." If I offer to weed the garden, she says, "Oh, no, dear, I always do that." She even makes my bed! I hope I don't die of boredom before school starts!

Sheila

		Ralph	**Sheila**
1.	Where is each friend staying?	_____	_____
2.	What is each friend's problem?	_____	_____
3.	Describe in one word how each friend feels.	_____	_____
4.	How does each friend's letter end?	_____	_____

- ☐ I can look back at the text to find answers.
- ☐ I can explain how characters' actions affect the story.
- ☐ I can compare and contrast themes, settings, and plots of stories that have something in common.

Now and Then

Read the passage.

There are about 600 million cars around the world. Cars first became popular in the early 1900s. Many early cars were built in a factory owned by a man named Henry Ford. He made cars that were low enough in price that many people could afford them.

Ford's cars looked different from the cars you see on the road now. Many were convertibles. The top folded up or down. There were only two seats in the car. There was one long seat in the front and one long seat in the back. Also, many of the cars did not have bumpers or mirrors. That's because those things cost extra money. Adding them made a car more expensive.

There were other differences too. Ford's cars used gas. But, the gas tank was under the driver's seat. That meant people had to lift the seat to put gas in the car. Sometimes, the cars would not start in cold weather. To get them to start, people poured hot water under the hood.

Today, cars are very different. They are more complicated and look more modern. Cars from long ago could not go as fast as the cars we drive today. But, they look like a lot of fun to ride!

Number the sentences from 1 to 5 in the order the details were presented in the passage. Use them to complete a summary of the passage on another sheet of paper.

_____ a.   Cars today are much faster than cars from the past.

_____ b.   Henry Ford made cars that many people could afford.

_____ c.   Cars first became popular in the early 1900s.

_____ d.   The gas tank of Ford's cars was under the driver's seat.

_____ e.   Ford's cars looked different from the cars of today.

❑   I can tell the main idea and supporting details of a text.
❑   I can describe the relationship between ideas using key words to show time, sequence, and cause and effect.

The Big Game

Read the story. Answer the questions about it on page 31.

Cranebrook Heights and Mareville were different neighborhoods. Cranebrook was near the river. Mareville was close to the woods. But, the communities had two important things in common.

The first was a big park. It had been there forever. It sat right in the middle of the two neighborhoods. The park had a huge soccer field, which was the second thing the neighborhoods had in common. Cranebrook kids and Mareville kids loved soccer.

One hot summer, things got tense. Here and there a word would get said. There was talk about how one neighborhood was better than the other. The leader of the Cranebrook kids was a boy named Peter. Katya was the one the Mareville kids all listened to. One day, Peter and Katya met in the park.

"We have to do something," Peter said. He wiped the back of his neck. "If this summer gets any hotter, things will explode."

Katya had a soccer ball. She kicked it to Peter. "I know. But, what can we do about it?"

They played for a half hour. At the end, they were hot and tired—but happy.

"Hey," Katya said. "I think I've got an idea." Katya told Peter her idea. They could have a big soccer game. That would help bring everyone together. They could have grown-up referees from both neighborhoods. That way, the game would be fair.

"I like it," Peter said. "But will it really work?"

For the next two weeks, all anyone talked about was the big game. Both teams practiced whenever they could. The game would decide who would win the honor of best team.

Then, a remarkable thing happened. Both sides practiced in the park each day. But, when Cranebrook Heights players saw Mareville players, they did not argue or fight. Instead, they high-fived each other. "Working hard?" they would say to one another. They all had something to do and something to look forward to.

When game day came, the August day was hotter than ever. Families came to watch from all over the city. The game was fierce. Cranebrook scored an early point. Then, Mareville tied the score. Mareville got ahead. But, in the last minute, Cranebrook scored another goal. The teams were tied!

There were only minutes left in the game. Would one of the teams score a winning goal? As a buzzer sounded, the game was over. The score was tied 3 to 3. No one had won! But, it did not matter. They all enjoyed the game.

Peter went over to Katya. "I never thought I'd see it," Peter said. "It's like we're all from the same neighborhood." Katya smiled. "I think today we are," she said.

☐ **I can read and comprehend grade-level fiction texts.**

The Big Game (cont.)

Circle the correct word or phrase in each blank to complete each sentence. Then, answer the questions about the story on page 30.

1. There were two neighborhoods. One, called_____ Cranebrook Heights / Mareville _____, was near

    a river. The other, called _____ Cranebrook Heights / Mareville _____, was near the woods.

    But, all of the kids in both places loved the same thing— _____ playing soccer / eating candy _____.

    They also shared a big _____ beach / park _____.

2. Why did Peter and Katya decide to have a soccer game? _____

    _____

3. Who won the game? _____

    _____

4. What lesson did the kids learn that summer? _____

    _____

☐ I can ask and answer questions about a text I have read.
☐ I can look back at a text to find the answers.
☐ I can retell stories using details and use them to understand the main idea.

It's What?

Read the story. Answer the questions about it on page 33.

Last Friday began as any other normal day during summer vacation. My little sister Makayla and I scrambled out of bed. We got dressed and quickly ate our breakfast. Then, we darted out the door.

The first thing we did was bounce on our new trampoline. Makayla and I have both improved. We are learning to perfect our knee drops.

Soon we lost interest and decided to in-line skate. We strapped on our helmets. Mine is an awesome purple and Makayla's is electric green. Then, we fastened our elbow and knee pads and tightened the buckles on our blades. I called out, "Let's roll!" Several neighbors joined us, including our friend Sally. We pretended we were in a roller derby. Eventually, boredom struck. Once again, we decided to do something different.

Hopscotch sounded fun, so we gathered colored chalk and started to play. After my little sister won three games straight, Sally and I talked about what to do next.

The three of us tried jumping rope. But, Makayla kept messing up. She complained that I was not twirling the rope correctly. So, we hung the jump rope on a hook in the garage. As Sally headed for home, my sister and I plopped down on the front porch steps.

"Summer is so-o-o-o-o boring," I said quite wearily.

"There is never anything fun to do," Makayla added.

Soon, we started to get hungry. "We'd better go inside and see what Mom has made for our lunch," I declared. We ran to the kitchen.

"Mom, what's for lunch?" asked Makayla.

Mom answered, "It's macaroni and cheese. I decided to make your favorite lunch because you know what happens next week."

"Huh?" I groggily replied, scratching my head. "What's happening next week?"

"School begins on Monday," reminded Mom.

Makayla and I froze in our tracks. "But, Mom," I whined. "There's so much more we have left to do this summer!"

Makayla and I looked at each other. Reality set in. We loved summer. We could not believe it was over already.

☐ **I can read and comprehend grade-level fictional texts.**

It's What? (cont.)

Read this summary of the story on page 32. Draw a line through any sentences that may be interesting but are not needed to retell the story. Then, answer the questions,

Last Friday, my sister Makayla and I woke and got ready to play. We ate our favorite energy-boosting breakfast.

The first thing we did was jump on the trampoline. We jumped very high and improved our drops.

When that became boring, we gathered some neighbors and began to in-line skate. It was fun to pretend we were competing in a roller derby. I just love to "lead the pack" around the block.

Next, we chose to hopscotch. This is Makayla's favorite activity because she always seems to win. I lost interest quickly because I always seem to lose. Maybe a lucky rock would help me.

Once again, we became bored, so we sat on the front porch. Soon, it was time for lunch. Our friend Sally went home and we walked into our kitchen. Mom had made our favorite meal. I could eat macaroni and cheese almost any time. Makayla loves it too.

Then, Mom announced that school begins next week. Thoughts of all we had left to do during our vacation floated through our minds.

1. How does the author feel about summer vacation in paragraph 6? _____

2. How does the author feel about summer vacation in paragraph 14? _____

3. What caused the change in the author's feelings? _____

   _____

4. Makayla said, "There is never anything fun to do." Explain why this is an example of hyperbole or exaggeration. _____

   _____

5. Number the events in the correct order.

   _____ The girls jumped rope.

   _____ The girls ate breakfast.

   _____ The girls went in-line skating.

   _____ Mom made macaroni and cheese.

   _____ Mom said that school starts next week.

   _____ The girls get bored.

   _____ The girls ran out the door.

   _____ The girls have so much left to do.

☐ I can look back at the text to find answers.
☐ I can explain how characters' actions affect the story.
☐ I can figure out the meaning of words and phrases in a story.
☐ I can separate literal from nonliteral language.

The Babysitting Blues—Chapter One

Read the first part of the story. Complete the activities on page 35.

Mrs. Bradford smiled broadly as she let me in the house. "Cassie, you don't realize how grateful Mr. Bradford and I are to see you! We know you have finals at the community college. We were afraid we wouldn't be able to get a babysitter on such short notice. We'll be home around midnight. Here's a list of instructions and an emergency number to call if necessary."

"Bye, Bettie!" Mr. and Mrs. Bradford both said. "Be sure to listen to Cassie!" They kissed their daughter on the cheek and left.

After they left, I read Mrs. Bradford's note. It said:

Cassie,

1. Warm spaghetti in the microwave and feed Bettie.

2. Give Bettie a bath and put on her pajamas.

3. Play a game with Bettie.

4. Put Bettie to bed.

5. Relax and watch television until we return.

"Simple enough," I thought as I put the note down and headed for the kitchen to feed Bettie.

I found the spaghetti in the refrigerator. As I placed the container in the microwave, little Bettie stood in front of the open refrigerator and put her hands in a bowl of chocolate pudding. "No, Bettie!" I said firmly as I pulled her away.

"Cassie want some?" Bettie asked as she laid her hands on my mouth and all across my face. I knew she was trying to be nice, but she still made a mess.

I quickly wiped her hands and my face and lowered her into her chair. After heating the spaghetti, I began to feed her dinner.

"Ooh, yummy, yummy!" Bettie clearly loved to eat spaghetti. She loved it so much that she grabbed some off her plate and threw it into the air! It landed everywhere, including my hair.

"Uh-oh," Bettie said with a big smile.

❑   **I can read and comprehend grade-level fiction texts.**

The Babysitting Blues—Chapter One (cont.)

"Bettie! Come back!" I yelled as I chased her into the living room, leaving a trail of spaghetti as I went. I finally caught her at the piano rubbing her hands across the keys. She said she wanted to play a song for me because she liked me so much. I thought that was nice. But, she left spaghetti all over the piano. That meant I had even more mess to clean up!

I carried Bettie back to the kitchen and fed her the little bit of spaghetti left in the bowl. Then, I checked the first item off Mrs. Bradford's list. Next on the list was Bettie's bath. She certainly needed one. This time I was not going to let her out of my sight.

1. Describe Cassie.

   _____

   _____

   _____

   _____

2. Describe Bettie.

   _____

   _____

   _____

   _____

3. Write a brief summary of the three ways that Bettie created mischief for Cassie.

   a. _____

   b. _____

   c. _____

Now, read chapter two of the story!

☐   I can describe characters in a story.
☐   I can explain how characters' actions affect the story.

The Babysitting Blues—Chapter Two

Read the next part of the story. Complete the activities on page 37.

I carried Bettie while I got a towel and her pajamas. I even held her while I ran the bath water. I poured a small amount of bubble bath into the tub. As I lowered Bettie into the water, she grabbed the bubble bath. Then, she dumped the whole thing into the tub! "Oh, well," I thought. "At least she'll get really clean."

Soon, bubbles were everywhere! Bettie splashed and splashed until everything was wet. Next, I rinsed off Bettie, took her out of the tub, and dried her. Finally, I put on her pajamas. Then, I checked off the second item on my list.

"Hmmm," I wondered as I checked the list again. "What kind of game should we play?"

"Cassie build a house!" Bettie shouted.

"OK, Bettie," I agreed, "but you have to sit perfectly still!" I was surprised that she listened as I used blocks to build four walls around her. "This was pretty easy," I thought.

But I had spoken too soon. Bettie suddenly stood up. "Let me help!" Bettie yelled. "I take house apart." Then, she kicked the blocks and sent them flying around the room.

I groaned as I checked item number three from my list. Then, I told her, "It's time for bed." I carried Bettie to her bedroom. Amazingly, she fell asleep right away. She must have been really tired after making all that mess.

After Bettie was asleep, I cleaned and cleaned until all of the mess was gone. It took hours. When I finally finished, I plopped down on the sofa. Just then, I heard the front door open.

"Cassie, we're back," said Mr. Bradford.

"The house looks great!" said Mrs. Bradford. "By the way, we would like to know if you can come back again tomorrow."

"Uh, I don't think so, Mrs. Bradford. I'm pretty busy." I felt badly that I couldn't help them out. But I just couldn't babysit Bettie again.

☐ **I can read and comprehend grade-level fiction texts.**

The Babysitting Blues—Chapter Two (cont.)

Answer the questions about the stories on pages 34, 35, and 36.

1. Briefly summarize three times that Bettie created mischief for Cassie in chapters one and two.

   a. _____

   _____

   b. _____

   _____

   c. _____

   _____

2. How did Cassie's attitude change from Chapter One to Chapter Two? _____

   _____

   Why did her attitude change? _____

   _____

3. Why did Cassie clean the house after Bettie went to bed? _____

   _____

4. How did the text box on page 34 help you understand the story? _____

   _____

5. Write a list of helpful babysitting tips for Cassie. _____

   _____

   _____

☐ I can ask and answer questions about a text I have read.
☐ I can explain how characters' actions affect the story.
☐ I can describe how the parts of a text build upon each other.
☐ I can explain how the illustrations support the text.

Growing Up

Read the story. Complete the activity on page 39.

By the time he was nine years old, Joey thought he had outgrown most of his toys. He decided to sell them at his family's garage sale. Joey started to clean his room, first going through his bedroom closet.

"I remember this old truck," he said to himself. "Grandpa and Grandma gave it to me when I turned five. I think Grandpa had as much fun as I did. We used it to dump sand in the sandbox. The truck got a little rusty, but it always worked fine."

Joey put the truck into a bag and pushed aside some clothes. He uncovered a shiny, blue and white yo-yo. "I remember thinking this yo-yo was broken when I first tried it," Joey recalled. "Then I practiced and realized nothing was wrong with it." He had even taught his younger brother Josh a few tricks with it. Little by little, the bag on the floor began to fill up.

Finally, at the bottom of the closet, was his well-worn teddy bear, Herbie. "I know I'm definitely too old for this!" Joey said to himself. "Teddy bears are for little kids." Joey picked up Herbie and dropped him into the bag of unwanted toys.

Joey leaned up against the bed to look over what he had collected. He stared inside the bag, and his eyes focused on Herbie. "Herbie and I had a lot of fun together," Joey recalled. "I remember when Dad, Mom, and Josh brought him to the hospital when I had my tonsils removed. My throat was sore, and I was so scared. And Herbie sure knew how to make me feel better during storms. When lightning and thunder woke me up I would pull the covers over my head. Then, I would hug Herbie so I wouldn't feel scared."

Joey gazed at Herbie one more time and then began thinking about other items in the bag. "Actually, maybe I'm not too old for these things. After all, they're still in pretty good shape!"

He carried the bag to his closet, dumped its contents in the back, and then grabbed the yo-yo. "Hey, Josh!" he called to his older brother. "Let's play with my yo-yo. Maybe I can teach you a few new tricks."

❑ **I can read and comprehend grade-level fiction texts.**

Growing Up (cont.)

Choose words from the word bank to complete a summary of the story on page 38. You may need to use some words more than once.

Word Bank

broken	friend	grandparents	keep	look
old	sell	truck	teddy bear	yo-yo

Joey felt that he was too _____ for most of his toys. So, he decided

to _____ them. He began to _____ through his closet.

First, Joey found an old _____ that his _____

had given him. Next, he discovered a _____. He had thought it was

_____ until he learned how to use it. Finally, Joey pulled out an

old _____. It had been his best _____ when he was a

little boy. After thinking about it, Joey decided to _____ his old

toys for a while. He realized that maybe he was not too _____

for them after all.

What would you do if you were Joey? Why? _____

_____

_____

_____

☐   **I can look back at the text to find answers.**
☐   **I can retell stories using details and use them to understand the main idea.**
☐   **I can compare my point of view to that of the narrator or characters.**

You Need a Wuzzy Pet!

Read the advertisement. Answer the questions about it on page 41.

You Need a Wuzzy Pet!

You do not need an animal to experience the joy of having a pet. Just get a Wuzzy Pet! It feels warm and fuzzy when you hold it. That is what makes it a "Wuzzy." A Wuzzy Pet always comes when you call. Plus, you never have to feed or bathe it. Your Wuzzy Pet will even do tricks, like roll over or sit down. And, it makes real animal noises. Choose your favorite. Get a Wuzzy Dog, a Wuzzy Cat, a Wuzzy Bird, or a Wuzzy Monkey. Or, collect them all!

Wuzzy Pets are even better than the real thing. Now available at a toy store near you!

(Prices may vary. Some assembly required. Batteries are not included. To avoid electric shock, do not spill liquids on the toy or place it in water.)

I can read and comprehend grade-level fiction texts.

You Need a Wuzzy Pet! (cont.)

Answer the questions about the advertisement on page 40.

1. What is this advertisement trying to sell you?

_____

_____

2. What does the advertisement say is good about the product?

_____

_____

3. What does the advertisement say is bad about the product?

_____

_____

4. Do you agree with the author? Why or why not?

_____

_____

5. What does the advertisement warn about the product?

_____

_____

6. Write a short summary of this advertisement.

_____

_____

_____

☐   I can look back at the text to find answers.
☐   I can retell stories using details and use them to understand the main idea.
☐   I can compare my point of view to that of the narrator or characters.
☐   I can use text features to locate important information.

Picture Time

Read the story. Complete the activities on page 43.

The time had come for the big class photo. Mr. Hallam, the photographer, had already done individual pictures of the fourth graders. He thought the last class would be a snap, as he liked to say. But, things did not go exactly as planned.

Ms. Gupta called out to her class. "Now, you each have a brush or a comb. Please use them to get ready for the picture." The students fidgeted as they all got ready.

Suddenly, the fire alarm sounded. "OK, everyone," Ms. Gupta said. "That means we're having a fire drill. You know what to do." With Ms. Gupta in the lead, the students filed out of the classroom. Mr. Hallam was right behind.

As they stepped outside in the sunny day, Mr. Hallam got an idea. "Hey, this would be the perfect place to take a picture," he told Ms. Gupta. "What do you think?"

"Sounds like a great idea to me," she replied.

So, all of the fourth graders got together to take the picture. But, just as Mr. Hallam held up his camera, a breeze began to blow. It blew everyone's hair out of place. The picture was ruined!

"Well, that didn't work," Mr. Hallam said. "Can you all fix your hair again?" The students did. They took out their brushes and combs. They straightened their hair and fixed their ribbons. Then, they got ready to take another picture.

But, as Mr. Hallam held up his camera, a breeze began to blow again. This time, it was even stronger. It blew everyone's hair out of place again. It also swirled fallen leaves into the air. They blew all around in front of the students. The picture was ruined again!

"Can we try one more time?" Mr. Hallam asked. "The third time will be the charm."

The students took out their combs and brushes one last time. They straightened their hair and fixed their ribbons. They smoothed down their curls and tightened their braids. Then, they got ready to take another picture.

But, as Mr. Hallam held up his camera, a breeze began to blow again. It was even stronger than the first time. It blew everyone's hair. It swirled fallen leaves into the air. It even scattered a flock of birds from a nearby tree. The breeze made a great big mess!

Everything looked so crazy, the students started to laugh. They all laughed and laughed. They looked like they were having such a fun time. Mr. Hallam thought, "What a great picture that would make." So, he held up his camera and finally snapped the picture.

Everyone loved the way the picture turned out. It was not a perfect photo. But, it was the most fun out of all of the fourth grade pictures.

☐ **I can read and comprehend grade-level fiction texts.**

Picture Time (cont.)

Answer the questions about the story on page 42.

1. In paragraph one, Mr. Hallam liked to say "the last class would be a snap." What does he mean when he says this? _____

   Why do you think he likes to say this? _____

2. What is the climax of this story? _____

   _____

   _____

   _____

Number the sentences in order from 1 to 10 to complete a summary of the story.

_____ a. Mr. Hallam finally snaps the picture.

_____ b. Everyone loves the photo of Ms. Gupta's class.

_____ c. A strong breeze begins to blow for the second time.

_____ d. Everyone's hair gets messy for the first time.

_____ e. Leaves swirl into the air.

_____ f. The school fire alarm goes off.

_____ g. A flock of birds scatters from a tree.

_____ h. Students comb their hair in the classroom.

_____ i. Mr. Hallam decides to take the picture outside.

_____ j. The class leaves the school and goes outside.

☐ I can retell stories using details and use them to understand the main idea.
☐ I can figure out the meaning of words and phrases in a story.
☐ I can separate literal from nonliteral language.
☐ I can use proper terms to name parts of text.

Helen Keller

Read the passage. Answer the questions about it on page 45.

Helen Keller was a well-known woman. She was born in 1880. When she was just 19 months old, she became very sick. Her illness left her blind and deaf. That meant that she was unable to see or hear. Her world became a dark, quiet place. She began to feel angry and afraid. As a result, she started to have temper tantrums and act wildly.

Helen's parents wanted to help her. They hired a teacher named Annie Sullivan. Annie understood what it meant to be blind. She found a way to teach Helen. Annie taught Helen to "hear" and "speak" with her hands. Helen even learned how to use her voice and speak.

Helen was very smart and dedicated. She became a very good student. She went to college and graduated with honors. When she became an adult, Helen wrote books and gave many speeches.

Helen Keller also worked to help others. She taught other people how to cope with being blind or deaf. She also worked against unfairness and violence. Helen won awards for all of the good things she did. She became very famous and lived to be 88 years old.

☐ I can read and comprehend grade-level informational texts.

Helen Keller (cont.)

Answer the questions about the passage on page 44.

1. What is the most important idea in this passage?

   a. Helen Keller learned how to hear and speak with her "hands."

   b. Helen Keller wrote books and gave speeches.

   c. Helen Keller became sick when she was 19 months old.

2. How did an illness affect Helen Keller?

   _____

3. Who helped Helen Keller learn how to speak?

   _____

4. Write a short summary of the passage.

   _____

   _____

   _____

   _____

5. In the second paragraph, why do you think "hear" and "speak" are in quotation marks?

   _____

6. What is the author's opinion of Helen Keller? _____

   _____

   Do you agree? Why or why not? _____

   _____

   _____

   _____

☐ I can tell the main idea and supporting details of a text.
☐ I can figure out the meaning of words and phrases in informational text.
☐ I can tell the difference between my own point of view and the author's point of view in informational text.

Name_____

The Giant Sequoia

Read the passage. Pay attention to the underlined words. Use them to complete the activities on page 47.

There are <u>forests</u> of <u>giant</u> trees in California. They are known as <u>sequoia</u> or redwood trees. A giant redwood can grow almost 76 meters (250 feet) tall. That is as big as a skyscraper!

Giant redwoods can live for thousands of years. For the first 250 years, they look like small pine trees. When they are about 500 years old, they reach their full height. Sequoias are not only <u>tall</u>, they are also wide. Some are as big as 8 meters (25 feet) wide. You could not wrap your arms around one of those trees!

The first giant redwoods started growing about 200 <u>million</u> years ago. They were probably around when dinosaurs walked the earth. There used to be a lot more giant redwoods. They once grew all over North America. But, then the weather turned cold for a while. These trees need warmth to grow. As a result, a lot of them died. Today, there are not many giant redwoods. They mainly grow in the <u>warm</u>, sunny state of California.

Forest fires are usually bad for trees. But, they sometimes help giant redwoods. The fire burns the small trees that grow in the shade of giant trees. That helps the small sequoia seedlings grow better. This way, they get more sunlight and water. Before a fire, these growing redwoods have to share sun and water with other small trees.

Also, the heat of a forest <u>fire</u> opens up the cones that grow high up in the trees. The cones contain seeds. When the cones open, the seeds fall to the ground. They land in the soil and grow into new redwood trees.

When a giant sequoia dies, it falls onto the forest floor. Animals build homes in the fallen tree. As the tree breaks down, it helps other plants grow. Even though the tree has died, it is still an important part of the forest. Giant redwoods are some of the most amazing trees on Earth!

☐ **I can read and comprehend grade-level informational texts.**

The Giant Sequoia (cont.)

Answer the questions about the passage on page 46.

1. What kind of text structure is used in this article? Circle all that apply.

   comparison   sequence   cause/effect

2. Why are forest fires good for sequoias? _____

   _____

   _____

3. What is the author's opinion about sequoias? Do you agree? _____

   _____

   _____

4. Write a summary of the passage on page 46. Your summary should include all of the underlined words from the passage.

   _____

   _____

   _____

   _____

   _____

   _____

   _____

   _____

   _____

   _____

☐ I can tell the main idea and supporting details of a text.
☐ I can describe the relationship between ideas using key words to show time, sequence, and cause and effect.
☐ I can use sentences and paragraphs to figure out the text structure.

How Was Your Trip?

Read the postcards Amy received over summer vacation. Fill in the chart to contrast her friends' vacations.

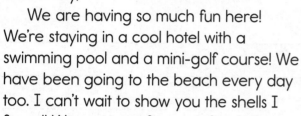

Dear Amy,

　　We are having so much fun here! We're staying in a cool hotel with a swimming pool and a mini-golf course! We have been going to the beach every day too. I can't wait to show you the shells I found! We went out for a seafood dinner last night. See you when I get back!

　　　　　　　　JoAnn

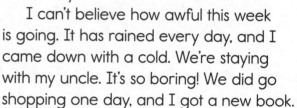

Dear Amy,

　　I can't believe how awful this week is going. It has rained every day, and I came down with a cold. We're staying with my uncle. It's so boring! We did go shopping one day, and I got a new book.

　　See you soon (I hope!),

　　　　　　　　Maria

	JoAnn	Maria
Where is each girl staying?	a.	b.
How does each girl feel about her trip?	c.	d.
List one thing each girl did while she was gone.	e.	f.
Describe the souvenir each girl is bringing home.	g.	h.

☐　I can compare and contrast themes, settings, and plots of stories that have something in common, such as the same author.
☐　I can read and comprehend grade-level fiction texts.

Kids Count!

Read the newspaper article. Answer the questions.

Student Volunteers Make a Difference

GREENE, MA Annabelle Davis and Antonio Grillo both volunteer for our town. Here is how these two students help:

Each spring, Annabelle works with her mother. She helps raise funds for a community garden. In the summer, Annabelle volunteers 10 hours a week. She works at the garden. She helps older gardeners weed. She waters the garden. She also looks after younger children. That gives their parents time to work in the garden.

Antonio visits retirement homes. These homes are in the Greene area. He makes two visits a month. He spends time talking with the people who live in the homes. He also plays the piano and puts on magic shows. Everyone looks forward to Antonio's lively visits. He makes these visits with his father.

Annabelle and Antonio

1. Where does Annabelle do her volunteer work?_____

_____

2. Where does Antonio do his volunteer work? _____

3. Who does volunteer work all year long? _____

4. Who does volunteer work mostly in the summer? _____

5. Whose volunteer work is done outdoors? _____

6. If Annabelle looked for a new volunteer job, which one do you think she would pick?

hospital assistant   nature center guide

7. If Antonio had time to teach other students, which subject do you think he would pick?

swimming   piano   karate

☐   I can ask and answer questions about a text I have read.
☐   I can look back at the text to find answers.
☐   I can describe characters in a story.

Name_____

Sara's Sweet Grass

Read the story. Complete the activities on page 51.

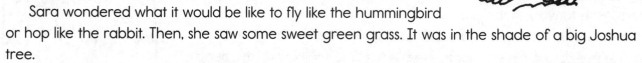

The first pink of the Mojave Desert dawn showed at the opening of Sara's burrow. She was hungry. It was time to go out and find some fresh grass to eat. Maybe there would even be a few wild poppies left.

Many other animals were out enjoying the cool March morning. A hummingbird whizzed by on his way to the flower fields down the hill. A cottontail bunny stopped to look at Sara. His nose twitched. Then he hopped away.

Sara wondered what it would be like to fly like the hummingbird or hop like the rabbit. Then, she saw some sweet green grass. It was in the shade of a big Joshua tree.

The grass was not close, but it was not that far away. If Sara kept going she would have plenty of time. She could eat and get back to her burrow before the sun got too hot.

A pack rat dashed past Sara. His cheeks were full of food. Sara put one foot in front of the other. She stopped and rested when she got tired. She crossed the place where a small stream had run when it rained in January. The water had been refreshing. She remembered the long drinks she had taken. It had been worth waking up from her winter sleep.

Sara climbed over a rock carefully. Having a shell was good protection, but if she ended up on her back, it would be hard to turn over again. The grass was close now. She took her first bite. She did not care if she could not fly or hop or run. She had eaten green grass every spring for 60 years and it was always good.

☐ **I can read and comprehend grade-level fiction text.**

Sara's Sweet Grass (cont.)

A girl named Katy lives in a desert town not far from Sara's home. In some ways, Katy's life is like Sara's. In other ways, their lives are very different. Read each pair of sentences. If they tell how Sara's life is the same as Katy's, circle the word **same**. If they tell how Sara's life is different from Katy's, circle the word **different**.

1. Sara is a desert tortoise. Katy is a girl.   same   different

2. Sara lives in a burrow. Katy lives in a house.   same   different

3. Sara eats in the morning. Katy does too.   same   different

4. Sara can live more than 60 years. Katy can too.   same   different

5. At what time of day does Sara go looking for food? _____

    Why does she go during this time? _____

6. Where is Sara? _____

7. How old is Sara? _____

8. Why is flipping over dangerous for Sara? _____

    _____

9. How did the illustrations help you better understand the story? _____

    _____

☐   I can look back at the text to find answers.
☐   I can describe characters in a story.
☐   I can explain how illustrations support the text.
☐   I can compare and contrast themes, settings, and plots of stories.

Special Days

Read the passage. Answer the questions about it on page 53.

July 4 is an American holiday. It is Independence Day. On July 4, 1776, America became a new country. It was no longer a part of England. On this day people celebrate freedom. There are parades. Many people watch fireworks. Flags are flown. **Independence** means to be on your own and take care of yourself. That is how the day got its name.

Canada also has an Independence Day. Canada became free from France on July 1, 1867. Canada became a new country. In Canada, this day is also called Canada Day. Fireworks and concerts are enjoyed on this day. July 1 is a day of firsts in Canada. It is a day of new things. The first radio network opened July 1, 1927. The first TV show was seen across Canada on July 1, 1958.

☐ **I can read and comprehend grade-level informational texts.**

Special Days (cont.)

Answer the questions about the passage on page 52.

1. What is being compared in the passage?

    a. freedom in America

    b. Independence Day in America and Canada

    c. radio and television in America and Canada

2. What is the same in both America and Canada?

    a. Both countries celebrate on the same day.

    b. Both countries became free from France.

    c. Both celebrate with fireworks.

3. What does *independence* mean? _____

4. What are three ways people celebrate Independence Day in America?

    _____

    _____

    _____

5. What are two ways people celebrate Independence Day in Canada?

    _____

    _____

6. What is one way both countries celebrate Independence Day?

    _____

☐ I can describe the relationship between ideas using key words to show time, sequence, and cause and effect.

☐ I can figure out the meaning of words and phrases in informational text.

☐ I can use text features to locate important information.

Two Island Groups

Life on the Hawaiian Islands and the Solomon Islands is similar and yet very different. Which one would you like to call home? Study the chart of facts. In each row, circle the square with the condition you would choose for your island home. At the bottom of the chart, write the name of your favorite island group. Then, complete the activities on page 55.

	Hawaiian Islands	Solomon Islands
Major Islands	8 islands in the middle of the Pacific Ocean (an area of 6,423 square miles or 10,220 square kilometers)	5 larger islands and over 900 smaller islands and reefs, not far from Australia (a total area of 11,599 square miles or 18666 square kilometers)
Population In 2010	1,360,301 people living there (with an average of 211 people per square mile, much like a city)	510,000 people living there (with an average of only 19 people per square mile, a more rural lifestyle)
Languages Spoken	English is the official and most often spoken language.	English is the official language, but over 63 other languages are spoken on the islands.
Crops Grown/ Products Made	Pineapple, sugar, flowers, and macadamia nuts are the major crops grown on the islands.	Wood products, palm tree oil, bananas, chocolate, and pineapple are the major products and crops of the islands.
Largest Industry, Type of Work Done by Residents	tourist trade, coffee, sugar, and pineapple About one out of three people work serving tourists. Most Hawaiians live and work in the largest city.	farming and fishing Three out of four people work or live on farms and in small towns. One in four people cannot read. Children are not required to attend school.
Favorite Sports	surfing, swimming, boating, hiking, fishing	soccer, rugby, cricket, observing nature while diving and snorkeling
Climate and Weather	Tropical: warm, gentle winds, sunny skies all year, some rain October to March	Tropical: very warm with a lot of rain every month of the year, frequent winds
My Favorite Island Group Is		

☐ **I can read and comprehend grade-level informational texts.**

Name_____

Two Island Groups (cont.)

Complete the activities with information from the chart on page 54.

1. Write two sentences explaining how you chose your favorite island group on the last page. Your statements should include three things that you compared in making your choice.

_____

_____

_____

_____

2. Write two sentences comparing and contrasting the weather and climate of the two island groups. In your sentences, make sure you explain how the weather on the two island groups is similar and how it is different.

_____

_____

_____

_____

❑ I can describe the relationship between ideas using key words to show time, sequence, and cause and effect.

❑ I can use text features to locate important information.

❑ I can compare and contrast two informational texts on the same topic.

Whale or Fish?

Chu wants to know whether Moby, a sea creature at the aquarium, is a whale or just a large fish. Fill in the chart at the bottom of the page. Complete the activities on page 57 to help answer Chu's question about the sea creature.

Whales live in salt water. They are huge animals with smooth, rubbery skin. Their tails swing up and down while swimming. Even though they live in the water, whales breathe oxygen and have lungs. Instead of breathing through a nose, whales breathe through a blowhole. People locate a whale by seeing the spray from the blowhole. The females give birth to one baby at a time. Baby whales are fed milk like other mammals. Whales are warm-blooded. Their body temperature never changes. A thick layer of fat keeps the temperature of the whale's body consistent. This layer of fat is called **blubber**.

Fish are found in salt water and in freshwater. Fish come in all sizes. Sharks are the biggest fish. The biggest shark was about 65 feet (20 meters) long. Most are much smaller than whales. A fish's body is covered with bony scales. Fish have tail fins that are straight up and down. Fish swim by moving their tail fins from side to side. Fish have gills that are able to take oxygen out of the water. To stay alive the fish need the water. Fish are cold-blooded; their body temperature changes with the temperature of the water. Most fish lay eggs in the water. After a time, the eggs hatch. Most parent fish care for the eggs or the young.

	Whales	**Fish**
type of water		
skin		
tail moves		
breathing		
body temperature		

☐ I can use text and visuals to help me understand a topic.
☐ I can read and comprehend grade-level informational texts.

Whale or Fish? (cont.)

Compare the **Moby Facts** to the whale and fish facts on page 56. Put an **X** in front of the facts that can help Chu identify which group Moby belongs to.

Moby Facts

_____ 1. This type of animal may measure over 67 feet (20 meters) long.

_____ 2. Their brains are the largest of any animal.

_____ 3. Spray from a blowhole can be seen from far away.

_____ 4. The creature's teeth are over eight inches (20 centimeters) long.

_____ 5. It devours giant squid, whales, and fish.

_____ 6. A famous story tells of how the creature damaged and sank whaling ships with one downward slap of its huge tail.

_____ 7. During the 18th century these creatures were hunted for a waxy material their bodies produced. The wax, along with blubber, was used in making candles and soaps.

_____ 8. Blubber helps the animal's body temperature stay the same, even in cold water.

9. What is *blubber*? _____

10. Is Moby a whale or a fish? _____

☐ I can look back at the text to find my answers.
☐ I can figure out the meaning of words and phrases in informational text.
☐ I can use text features to locate important information.
☐ I can compare and contrast two informational texts on the same topic.

Mollusks

Read the passage. Complete the activity on page 59.

Bivalve

Gastropoda

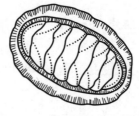

Chiton

Mollusks are animals with no backbone. Their soft bodies are usually covered by hard shells. On many beaches, you will find the shells. We call them seashells. Most of the shells you find on the beach are empty.

The mollusk family is divided into seven classes. Only some of them have hard shells. Gastropoda is one class of mollusks. Most gastropods have a single, coiled shell. Included in this class are limpets, slugs, and snails. They can be found in the Atlantic and Pacific Oceans in North America.

Bivalves make up another large class of mollusks. The shells of bivalves are two shells hinged together. The animals that call these shells home include clams, oysters, mussels, and scallops. They, too, are found on both coasts of North America.

A third class of mollusks are chitons. Their bodies are covered by eight shell plates. The plates look something like a turtle's shell. Bounded and mossy mopalia are all included in this class. Chitons live in shallow rock pools. They live along the Pacific Ocean from Alaska to Mexico.

❑   **I can read and comprehend grade-level informational texts.**

Mollusks (cont.)

Use information from the passage on page 58 to complete the chart and answer the questions.

	gastropods	bivalves	chitons
1. What do their shells look like?	a.	b.	c.
2. Where can they be found?	d.	e.	f.
3. List mollusks included in each group.	g.	h.	i.

4.   How did the illustrations help you understand the text? _____

_____

☐   I can ask and answer questions about an informational text.
☐   I can look back at the text to find my answers.
☐   I can use text features to locate important information.
☐   I can use text and visuals to help me understand a topic.

What Is a Platypus?

You may never see a platypus. But, as you read about the animal, you can picture it in your mind by comparing it with other animals. Underline the ways a platypus is like a duck in **red**. Underline the ways a platypus is like a beaver in **blue**. (Hint: Remember, a beaver is a mammal and a duck is a bird.) Use the passage to draw the missing body parts on the drawing. Complete the activities on page 61.

A platypus looks like a mix of a beaver and a duck. The male platypus has stingers like bees have. The stingers are in its rear feet and are used for protection. At first, scientists did not believe the platypus was real. They thought someone was trying to trick them.

A platypus hunts underwater, paddling with its webbed feet like a duck. A strong, flat tail steers it. The tail of a platypus looks much like a beaver's tail. A rubbery bill scoops up insects and shellfish from among the mud at the bottom. Mud and gravel come mixed with the food. Like a bird, a platypus does not have teeth. So, the gravel helps "grind" the food.

Platypuses build nests on or near the water. Unlike most other mammals, the platypus lays eggs. The female keeps the eggs warm with her velvety fur until they hatch. She then feeds the young milk, like other mammals.

I can read and comprehend grade-level informational texts.

What Is a Platypus? (cont.)

Use information from the passage on page 60 to help you label the diagram. Then, compare the facts about the platypus on the left to the list of animals on the right. In each space, write the letter of the word or phrase that completes the sentence.

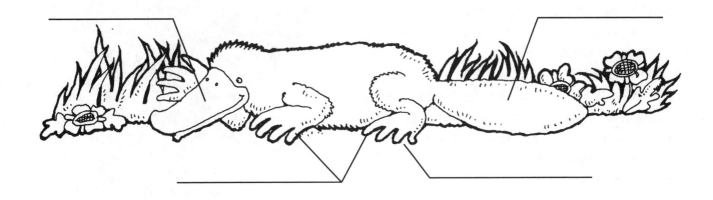

1. The platypus lays eggs like _____.

2. The platypus has a bill and webbed feet like _____.

3. The platypus swims with a long, flat tail like _____.

4. The platypus uses a stinger for protection like _____.

5. The platypus has no teeth like _____.

6. The platypus builds a nest on the ground near the water like _____.

7. The female platypus produces milk for its young like _____ .

a. a duck

b. a beaver

c. neither the duck nor the beaver

d. both the duck and the beaver

☐   I can look back at the text to find my answers.
☐   I can use text features to locate important information.
☐   I can use text and visuals to help me understand a topic.
☐   I can use sentences and paragraphs to figure out the text structure.

Name_____

Happy New Year!

Read the story. Answer the questions about it on page 63.

Jean's family lives in France. On New Year's Eve they have a huge supper. Jean gets to stay up late. At midnight, they kiss under the mistletoe. They also exchange holiday gifts.

Hua's family lives in China. On the Chinese New Year, the whole family has a big feast. Hua and the other children get "lucky money." The "money" is in red envelopes from their parents. Then, Hua and her family go out to a festival. Lines of dancers dance in the street in costumes. People set off firecrackers to welcome the new year.

Gary's family lives in the United States. On New Year's Eve, they host a party for family and friends. They have a big meal together. Then, they pop popcorn. Gary gets to stay up until midnight. Then, everybody throws confetti, blows noisemakers, and kisses each other.

❏ **I can read and comprehend grade-level fiction texts.**

Happy New Year! (cont.)

Use information from the story on page 62 to answer the questions. Put a **T** on the line before the statement if it is true, and an **F** on the line before the statement if it is false.

_____ 1.   All of the celebrations include a large meal.

_____ 2.   Jean's celebration includes firecrackers.

_____ 3.   Jean and Gary get to stay up late on New Year's Eve.

_____ 4.   Hua receives "lucky money" in red envelopes.

_____ 5.   Gary's family exchanges gifts as part of their celebration.

_____ 6.   Jean gets to see people dance in costumes at a festival.

_____ 7.   Hua's and Jean's families kiss at midnight.

_____ 8.   Gary's family throws confetti at midnight.

9.   How is the text on page 62 organized? (Circle one.)

comparison   cause and effect   sequence

10.   How is your New Year's Eve similar to and different from Gary's?

_____

_____

_____

_____

☐   **I can compare my point of view to that of the narrator or characters.**
☐   **I can compare and contrast themes, settings, and plots of stories.**

The Greatest Gift

Read the story. Answer the questions.

Rena brushed the color across the canvas. *I'll never be able to do it*, she thought. *I can't paint the picture of the woods.*

"Rena," said her art teacher. "What you've done here is beautiful! You have such talent. You're one of my best students because you have such an unusual style."

Rena shook her head. "Maybe, but my work will never look like that." She looked again at the painting hanging on the wall.

When Rena walked in the door at home, her little brother grabbed her by the arm. "Rena, Rena, will you make a picture for Grandpa's party? I wrote a poem for him, but I want to put it with a great big picture. And I want you to do it because you're such a great artist."

Rena smiled. "OK, Oscar. Grab all those old pictures from the box."

For weeks, Rena worked with her paints on a big canvas. She placed every stroke and chose every color with great care, looking at the old pictures as she worked.

At Grandpa's party, Oscar read his poem. Then, Rena gave Grandpa the painting. Tears filled Grandpa's eyes. "The poem was wonderful, and the painting. The painting shows my old friends and my old neighborhood in a way that makes me feel as though I'm there all over again. Rena, you've shown me how special all of these people have been in my life. You and Oscar are wonderful."

1. How would you describe Rena at the beginning of the story? _____

_____

_____

How would you describe her at the end of the story? _____

_____

_____

2. Why did Grandpa cry when he saw Rena's painting? _____

_____

_____

_____

☐ I can look back at the text to find answers.
☐ I can retell stories using details and use them to understand the main idea.
☐ I can describe characters in a story.

Light the Lights!

Read the story. Answer the questions about it on page 66.

Chapter 1

Jana scrunched her nose and dove into her bed. *Not tomorrow*, she thought. *The science fair cannot be tomorrow!* Jana knew she'd have to give the speech she had prepared to go with her science fair project. She was terrified to speak in front of big crowds. Just thinking about the report made her heart beat faster.

Jana's sister Yolanda burst into her room. "Did you hear?" Yolanda shouted. "We could get a prize for our report tomorrow!"

"What do you mean?" asked Jana.

"The City Science Committee is going to all of the schools to listen to the reports. They're going to give a big cash prize to the people who win."

"Our family could really use that money," Jana said. "Linda will be finished with high school soon, and the money could help her pay for college."

Chapter 2

The next day, Jana and Yolanda set up the equipment to prepare for the report. Jana asked Yolanda to connect all of the wiring because Yolanda worked well with electronics.

Jana opened her mouth to speak as Yolanda prepared to show the audience how the experiment worked, but not a single sound came from Jana's mouth. She felt sweat bead up on her palms. Her hands shook. Silence filled the room.

Our family needs the prize money, thought Jana. *I know I can do this.* Slowly, Jana began to speak. Her hands stopped shaking. She explained to the listeners that the lights in the experiment would light up because they received a charge from the batteries through the wiring. She explained how she and Yolanda had thought of the experiment.

The next day, Yolanda burst into Jana's room again. She was grinning from ear to ear because she was so happy. "Have you heard? It's the best of the best news! We won!"

"I knew we could do it," said Jana. She and Yolanda raced downstairs to tell their mom and dad and older sister.

❏   **I can read and comprehend grade-level fiction texts.**

Light the Lights! (cont.)

Use information from the story on page 65 to answer the questions.

1. Why is the information in Chapter 1 important to the story? _____

    _____.

2. How did Jana change from Chapter 1 to Chapter 2? _____

    _____.

3. Jana wanted to win the science competition because _____

    _____.

4. The day after the competition, Jana and Yolanda raced down the stairs because _____

    _____.

5. Write two ways Jana and Yolanda are alike. _____

    _____.

6. Write two ways Jana and Yolanda are different. _____

    _____.

7. Explain how Jana's fear of speaking affected the story._____

    _____.

8. What tips do you know to help Jana speak in front of groups? _____

    _____.

___

❏ I can use proper terms to name parts of text.
❏ I can describe how the parts build upon each other.
❏ I can compare my point of view to that of the narrator or characters.

Name_____

Out-of-This-World Vacation

Read the advertisement. Answer the questions.

Come join us . . .

. . . for a thrilling once-in-a-lifetime vacation! Hop aboard our luxury space liner and fly to the moon for an adventurous six-day vacation. We know you will love this one because you are thrill-seeking, fun-loving kinds of people. You will love the happy feeling of floating through the air. And, because there is no gravity, your luggage will feel as light as air. Since we will be approximately 221,456 miles (356,399 km) above Earth, you will find the view amazing. We hope you join us for this awesome trip.

Rules and Restrictions:
A charge of $8.4 million will be in place due to high fuel costs.

1. Why does the travel agency know people will love this vacation?

    _____

    _____

2. Why will travelers' luggage feel as light as air?

    _____

    _____

3. Why does the trip cost $8.4 million?

    _____

    _____

4. The author thinks everyone will enjoy this vacation. Why might someone not like this trip?

    _____

    _____

☐   **I can look back at the text to find answers.**
☐   **I can compare my point of view to that of the narrator or characters.**
☐   **I can read and comprehend grade-level fiction texts.**

How the World Wide Web Came to Be

Read the passage. Answer the questions.

In 1980, scientist Tim Berners-Lee was working with software in the Swiss Alps. He wanted to create a way to organize and find information, because it was hard to share information with scientists in different countries. He thought of the World Wide Web.

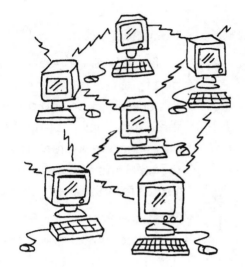

How did the World Wide Web get its name? Berners-Lee and a coworker tried to think of names. They could not come up with any ideas they liked. Because they needed a name quickly, they came up with the World Wide Web. This name described how information was passed around the world. They planned to think of another name later. However, the name caught on quickly and was never changed.

1. Why did Tim Berners-Lee come up with the idea for the World Wide Web?

   _____

   _____

   _____

2. Why did Tim Berners-Lee and a coworker decide to use the name World Wide Web? _____

   _____

   _____

3. Why do you think Tim Berners-Lee thought there needed to be a way to organize and find

   information? _____

   _____

   _____

☐ I can look back at the text to find my answers.
☐ I can describe the relationship between ideas using key words to show time, sequence, and cause and effect.
☐ I can tell the difference between my own point of view and the author's point of view.

Dancing in Rio

Read the story. Answer the questions about it on page 70.

Allen was upset. His parents said they had to go to a wedding in Brazil, and Allen had to go too. It meant two whole weeks away from his friends! Allen thought the wedding would be boring. What was so interesting about Brazil?

When he got to Rio, Allen realized the word boring did not fit anything! The whole country of Brazil was throwing a big party. The celebration was called Carnival. Rio was the center of the party.

There were people in bright clothes everywhere. Everyone danced in the streets. The music was loud and exciting. It made Allen want to dance with the crowd.

Allen was excited for other reasons too. When they left Wisconsin, it was snowing. Down in Brazil, it was summer! He could wear shorts and flip-flops.

"Don't go out of my sight!" his mom shouted. The same sights that made Allen happy seemed to make his mom nervous.

The music got louder. It made Allen's heart jump. Mary, his older sister, liked it too. Together, Allen and Mary danced with the music.

That night there was a party. It was for the bride and groom. Everyone was dancing. Allen's heart was still jumping. He watched Mary dance. His sister was good! The bride asked Allen to join them.

"Come out on the dance floor!" she said.

Allen was nervous. Everyone was watching him. He had never danced in front of an audience. No one had been watching him at Carnival.

"Allen, you were a good dancer today. Show everyone your dance steps!" Mary said.

That gave Allen courage. He went out onto the dance floor. Allen danced all night long. At the end of the night, the Brazilians cheered for him.

"You are the best of everyone," they said.

I can read and comprehend grade-level fiction texts.

Dancing in Rio (cont.)

Use the story on page 69 to complete the cause and effect statements.

1. Allen did not want to go to Brazil because _____

   _____ .

2. Rio did not seem boring because _____

   _____ .

3. Allen liked the music at Carnival because _____

   _____ .

4. Allen was nervous to dance with the bride and groom because _____

   _____ .

5. Allen stopped being nervous when _____ .

6. Do you think Allen had a good time? Why or why not? _____

   _____

   _____

7. Compare how Allen felt at the beginning of the story to how he felt at the end of the story.

   _____

   _____

   _____

- ☐ I can ask and answer questions about a text I have read.
- ☐ I can look back at the text to find answers.
- ☐ I can describe characters in a story.
- ☐ I can explain how characters' actions affect the story.

Prima Ballerina

Read the story. Complete the cause and effect statements.

Keisha loved to watch ballet because the dancers flew through the air. They made great leaps and jumps. One day, Keisha decided she wanted to be a ballerina. She practiced standing on her toes all day long. Nothing happened. She practiced leaping across the living room. Nothing happened. She even leaped off the couch! Keisha still did not feel like a ballerina.

Keisha was desperate. She wanted to be a ballerina more than anything else. Finally, she asked her mom to buy her a tutu. Surely that would mean she was a ballerina. She slipped on the tutu and waited. Nothing happened. Keisha sat down on the floor and cried. "Why can't I be a ballerina?" she asked.

Just then, Keisha's mom dropped a paper on her lap. It said *Madame Bleu's Ballerina School* on the front. Keisha beamed from ear to ear. Dance school would help her become a ballerina!

1. Keisha likes to watch ballet because _____

_____ .

2. Keisha practices standing on her toes and leaping because _____

_____ .

3. Keisha asks her mom to buy her a tutu because _____

_____ .

4. Keisha cries because _____

_____ .

5. Keisha smiles at the end of the story because _____

_____ .

☐   **I can look back at the text to find answers.**
☐   **I can explain how characters' actions affect the story.**
☐   **I can read and comprehend grade-level fiction texts.**

The Giant Wave

Read the passage. Complete the cause and effect statements.

Earthquakes make the earth shake. They can cause damage to houses. Do you know that earthquakes can cause tsunamis too?

A tsunami is a huge wave. When an earthquake happens, it can move ocean water. A tsunami can be 100 feet (31 m) tall! It can cause damage to houses near the beach.

Scientists want to save lives. They created the Pacific Tsunami Warning System. The system finds earthquakes in the ocean. It warns people that a big wave may be coming. People can seek safety before the wave hits.

1. What is a tsunami? _____

2. Tsunamis are caused by _____ .

3. A tsunami causes _____ .

4. Experts have created a warning system because _____

   _____ .

5. The warning system helps people because _____

   _____ .

6. Write a summary of this text.

   _____

   _____

   _____

   _____

☐   I can tell the main idea and supporting details of a text.
☐   I can describe the relationship between ideas using key words to show time, sequence, and cause and effect.
☐   I can figure out the meaning of words and phrases in informational text.

Look! Up in the Sky!

Read the passages. Answer the questions about them below and on page 74.

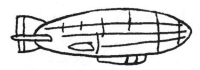

Lights in the Sky

An aurora borealis is one of the brightest nighttime lights people have ever seen. It can be caused by particles in the air that reflect light. It can also be caused by huge eruptions of gas on the sun. These eruptions are called solar flares. People often describe an aurora borealis as "light dancing across the sky."

1. How many effects are discussed in this paragraph? _____

2. Explain your answer. What are the effects? _____

_____

3. How many causes are discussed in this paragraph? _____

4. Explain your answer. What are the causes? _____

_____

Explosion in the Sky

In 1937, the Hindenburg airship exploded in the sky. For years, people argued about what caused the explosion. Hydrogen gas caused the airship to rise into the sky. At first, people thought that hydrogen gas had caused the explosion. Now, it is believed that a different chemical on the airship made it explode. The chemical might have been a powdered metal.

5. What did people first believe caused the explosion of the Hindenburg?

_____

_____

6. What did people later believe caused the explosion of the Hindenburg?

_____

_____

☐ I can look back at the text to find my answers.
☐ I can describe the relationship between ideas using key words to show time, sequence, and cause and effect.

Look! Up in the Sky! (cont.)

Use the passages on page 73 to answer the questions.

1. What is the main idea of "Lights in the Sky?" _____

   _____

2. What are two details that support the main idea?

   a. _____

   b. _____

3. What is the main idea of "Explosion in the Sky?" _____

4. What are two details that support the main idea?

   a. _____

   b. _____

5. Both of these texts are about events that happened in the sky. Complete the Venn diagram, comparing and contrasting these two texts.

Lights in the Sky   **Explosion in the Sky**

Both

☐ I can tell the main idea and supporting details of a text.
☐ I can compare and contrast two informational texts on the same topic.

Science Action

Read each description. Answer the questions on page 76.

Push Off

Fill a balloon with air. Hold the end closed and then let it go. The balloon will zoom forward as the air escapes. You pushed air into the balloon, and now the air pushes the balloon around as it comes back out.

Pull In

Because a magnet attracts some metals, it can pull a key toward it. A magnet will not pull a rubber band, because a rubber band is not magnetic. Only two magnetic objects will be attracted to each other.

Travel Across

Glaciers are large chunks of ice that slowly move over the land. Glaciers have an effect on the land as they travel. Because glaciers pick up parts of the land as they move, glaciers can carve out large areas. As glaciers melt, they leave behind bits of earth that can build up areas of land.

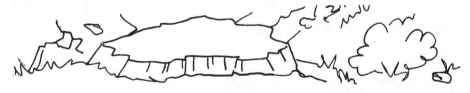

Circle Around

When the sun heats water, the water evaporates and forms vapor. The vapor forms clouds when it cools. The water droplets fall to the earth as rain. The rain evaporates, and the cycle begins again.

☐ **I can read and comprehend grade-level informational texts.**

Science Action (cont.)

Use the descriptions on page 75 to choose the correct answer to each question.

1. Glaciers change the land because

   a. there is an equal and opposite reaction for every action.

   b. water drops grow heavy.

   c. they pick up pieces of land as they move.

   d. they are frozen.

2. If you fill a balloon with air, hold the end, and let it go, it will zoom forward because

   a. it is frozen.

   b. a balloon is a law of motion.

   c. air pushes it.

   d. vapor forms clouds.

3. Water evaporates because

   a. the sun heats up the water.

   b. it is a law of motion.

   c. a magnet attracts metal.

   d. water drops grow heavy.

4. A magnet will pull a key in its direction because

   a. water drops grow heavy.

   b. the magnet and the key are both magnetic.

   c. a rubber band is not made of metal.

   d. it leaves behind something that has been frozen inside.

5. How did the illustrations help you understand the text?

   _____

   _____

   _____

❑   I can describe the relationship between ideas using key words to show time, sequence, and cause and effect.

❑   I can use text and visuals to help me understand a topic.

Washed Away

Read the passage. Answer the questions.

Erosion causes rocks and soil to be broken down. It can be caused by water, wind, ice, or gravity. People often think of erosion by water because it can be so noticeable. One famous example of erosion is Niagara Falls. These falls used to be 7 miles (11 km) away from their current position but have moved over the years because of erosion. Water and small pieces of rock have worn away the cliffs and caused the flow of water to slowly move backward. Because some of the rock is softer, it is worn away first. If you were to take all of the water away from the falls, you would see that the top of the rock sticks out farther than the bottom. This is because the bottom rock is softer.

Erosion is always at work. The more water that flows over rocks, the more the rocks erode. At Niagara Falls, they have tried to slow down the erosion by stopping some of the water from reaching the falls. So, only some of the water that should be eroding the rock is doing its job. However, the falls will continue to slowly erode. People can try to slow down erosion, but they will never stop it.

1. Why have the Niagara Falls moved?

   _____

   _____

2. Why does the top of Niagara Falls stick out farther than the bottom?

   _____

   _____

3. Why have people tried to stop water from going over the falls?

   _____

   _____

4. What do you think will eventually happen to Niagara Falls?

   _____

   _____

☐ I can describe the relationship between ideas using key words to show time, sequence, and cause and effect.

☐ I can tell the difference between my own point of view and the author's point of view in informational text.

☐ I can read and comprehend grade-level informational texts.

Time Travelers

Look at the comic and read the story. Circle the correct answers.

1. You can tell that

    a. the time machine is very advanced.

    b. Paige and Javon want to travel to the future.

    c. Paige and Javon know lots of history.

2. Another word for **product** is

    a. machine.

    b. result.

    c. cube.

3. To create their time machine, it took Paige and Javon

    a. less than an hour.

    b. about an hour.

    c. more than an hour.

4. How did the illustrations help you understand the text? _____

_____

☐ I can look back at the text to find answers.
☐ I can figure out the meaning of words and phrases in a story.
☐ I can explain how illustrations support the text.
☐ I can read and comprehend grade-level fiction texts.

TTay

Lost in Space

Look at the comic and read the story. Answer the questions.

The astronauts were headed to a new planet, but they made a wrong turn. They had to stop at a space station to ask for directions. They were not sure where they stopped, but there were some clues. They were on a large red planet, and the aliens called themselves Martians.

1.   On what planet did the astronauts stop?

Venus   Mars   Saturn

How do you know? _____

_____

_____

2.   To which planet did the astronauts want to go?

Venus   Mars   Saturn

How do you know? _____

_____

_____

☐   **I can explain how illustrations support the text.**
☐   **I can read and comprehend grade-level fiction texts.**

Name_____

Long Distance Show-and-Tell

Read the letters. Answer the questions.

April 2, 2015

Dear Omeka,

How is everything in New York? It's been just over a week, but I really miss you! Do you remember how we always talked about getting a pet? Well, here in Texas, I am finally able to have one. Wags is so much fun! He wags his tail every time he sees me. He curls up into a ball when he sleeps. He even plays fetch. You would think he was a dog! The only difference is, he does not bark. His meows are very loud though.

I can't wait for you to visit and meet Wags!

Your best friend,
Rachel

April 8, 2015

Dear Rachel,

It was great receiving your letter. Wags sounds really cool! During the summer, I hope to get acquainted with him. I just got a new pet too! Fluffy is so cute. She has the softest fur and such a bushy tail. I just love her long ears. I have so much fun watching her run and play. For now she sleeps in a little shoebox. When I visit you, I won't bring Fluffy. She hops away too easily. She might get lost on a Texas farm!

Write soon!

Love,
Omeka

1. Where is Rachel? _____ Where is Omeka? _____

2. Wags is a _____ . How do you know? _____

_____

3. Fluffy is a _____ . How do you know? _____

_____

☐ I can look back at the text to find answers.
☐ I can read and comprehend grade-level fiction texts.

Building Houses

Read the story. Answer the questions.

Tests of Building Materials

Our star reporter tested the quality of three housing materials. The results were shocking!

Straw was the weakest. Wind forces of only 10 mph left a small, straw house in disarray. "I wouldn't live in this type of house," the reporter said.

Next, he tested houses made of wooden sticks. Strong wind forces of 30 mph caused a stick dwelling to fall over. "Sticks may be popular with dogs, but they should not be used to build houses," the reporter said.

His final experiment tested bricks. "I found bricks to be sturdy. My many attempts to knock over the walls failed," the reporter said.

Please note: This assignment left our reporter a little winded. He will not be on assignment again until next month.

1. In the passage, what is another word for *house*?

   a. materials   b. dwelling   c. bricks   d. winded

2. If the prefix *dis-* means "not" and *array* means "to place in order," what does *disarray* mean?

   _____

3. Why did the reporter not want to live in a straw house?

   a. He does not like straw.

   b. It is not safe.

   c. He does not like wind.

4. The article's headline is not very interesting. Write a headline to capture the reader's attention.

   _____

5. On the back of this sheet of paper, compare and contrast "Tests of Building Materials" to "The Three Little Pigs."

☐   **I can compare and contrast themes, settings, and plots of stories.**

Tyler on the Mound

Read the story. Use context clues to infer the answers to the questions on page 83.

Tyler's stomach **lurched** as he opened the car door. He clutched his mitt and pulled on his ball cap. He looked anxiously at the diamond-shaped field where his teammates gathered. Tyler was the new pitcher for the Hawks. Braden, their former pitcher, moved away last week, and Coach asked Tyler to take his place on a trial basis. "Good grief!" Tyler said. "I'm the pitcher."

Tyler joined his teammates on the field for warm-ups and stretches. His eyes wandered to the area where their opponents, the Tigers, stretched and moved like large jungle cats. The Tigers were giants, and they had big muscles. They had to be a lot older than he was, Tyler was sure of it.

"What's wrong?" asked Jake, Tyler's best friend. "You look like you ate my sister's Eggplant Surprise. The surprise was she forgot to take it out of the oven when the timer buzzed. Yuck."

Tyler did not laugh at his friend's joke. "I haven't pitched before, not in a game!" he said. "If I make a mistake, we could lose!"

Jake scratched his head. "Same thing was true when you played right field. It didn't stop you from playing."

"I guess," Tyler said.

Tyler took his place on the pitcher's mound. Harsh stadium lights blocked out the stars, and the crowd roared in the stands. Even though the air was cool, sweat stung his eyes. He looked into the stands and saw his parents smile. He looked at the coach, and the coach gave him a serious nod, the sign to start the game. He looked at the boy at bat, and the boy glared back at him.

Tyler looked at Jake, who crouched behind home plate.

Jake gave Tyler a wide, goofy grin. "Come on, Ty! You can do it! Put it here." he yelled, holding his mitt as a target.

Tyler took a deep breath, wound up, and pitched. Swish! The batter swung and missed. Jake tossed the ball back to Tyler, and Tyler let the second pitch fly even faster. The batter swung so hard he spun around, but he didn't hit the ball, Tyler burned a third pitch directly across the plate. Whump! The ball struck Jake's mitt, and the umpire yelled, "You're out!" The batter **scowled**, dropped the bat, and returned to the dugout.

The next batter for the Tigers was even bigger than the first. He scowled at Tyler, but Tyler just smiled. His heart beat in a slow, steady rhythm as he focused his attention towards the plate.

□ **I can read and understand grade-level fiction texts.**

Tyler on the Mound (cont.)

Use information from the story on page 82 to answer the questions.

1. What game did Tyler play? _____

   How do you know? _____

   _____

2. What is the meaning of the word *lurch*?

   a. to sway or tip suddenly   c. to eat

   b. to walk around   d. to pitch a baseball

3. How did Tyler feel about pitching at first? _____

   How do you know? _____

   _____

4. How did Tyler feel about pitching at the end of the story? _____

   How do you know? _____

   _____

5. In paragraph 2, the author said the team moved like large jungle cats. What type of figurative language is this? _____

6. What metaphor does the author use in paragraph 2 to describe the size of the Tigers?

   _____

   _____

7. What is the meaning of the word *scowled*? _____

8. Find two examples of onomatopoeia in the passage.

   _____   _____

   ❑ **I can describe characters in a story.**
   ❑ **I can figure out the meaning of words and phrases in a story.**

Gardening with Garth

Read the article. Answer the questions on page 85.

The Midwest Advance

March 6, 2015

Do you like beans? Lots of beans? If so, this report will knock your socks off! While traveling through the Midwest, I met the world's best bean expert. His name is Jack, and he loves to grow bean plants. He especially loves growing lima beans, navy beans, kidney beans, and soybeans.

His plants are enormous. Most are so tall they must be tied to poles to stay up. Jack's plants appear to vanish among the clouds!

Jack has a lot of advice for farmers. He stresses that bean plants should be planted in rich, loose, warm soil. However, he refuses to share his special secret for such unbelievable plant growth.

As Jack's success becomes known around the country, many people will want to travel to see the beans. I advise travelers not to come by plane. The local airport is closed because of blockages in the sky. These blocks may or may not be related to the plants. However, it is well worth your time to find a different way to travel and visit!

For my next article, I am off to view a pumpkin patch. It is rumored that these pumpkins grow so big people actually live in them!

—Garth

☐ I can read and comprehend grade-level fiction texts.

Gardening with Garth

Answer the questions about the article on page 84. Some questions may have more than one answer.

1. *Do you like beans? Lots of beans? If so, this report will knock your socks off!*

    In this selection of text, what does the phrase *knock your socks off* mean? _____

    _____

2. Write one way this article is similar to the story "Jack and the Beanstalk." _____

    _____

    Write one way this article is different from the story "Jack and the Beanstalk." _____

    _____

3. Which of the following means of transportation would Garth suggest you use to visit Jack?

    a. car   b. jet   c. helicopter   d. bus

    How do you know? _____

    _____

    _____

4. Jack's plants

    a. are probably very strong.

    b. are probably taller than Jack's house.

    c. probably produce large beans.

    d. are similar to other bean plants.

    How do you know? _____

    _____

    _____

    _____

☐   I can figure out the meaning of words and phrases in a story.
☐   I can compare and contrast themes, settings, and plots of stories that have something in common, such as the same author.

Bear Scare

Read the play. Answer the questions on page 87.

Narrator: Ebony and her brothers, Darius and Forrest, sat around the campfire. The flames cast an eerie glow on Forrest's face as he told a story about a lost camper and a bear. The campfire crackled. Ebony shivered as red-gold embers floated skyward.

Forrest: Are you scared?

Ebony: *(Shakes her head.)* No, I'm just cold.

Darius: I'll get a blanket from the tent. *(He scampers off into the dark.)*

Ebony: Don't finish the story until Darius comes back.

Forrest: Are you sure you aren't scared?

Narrator: Ebony felt something fuzzy land on her head.

Darius: Grrrrrrrrrrr!

Narrator: Ebony jumped. Her head smacked into her brother's nose.

Darius: Ow!

Ebony: I'm sorry! You surprised me!

Narrator: Darius rubbed his nose and laughed.

Darius: I guess I deserved it.

Forrest: Should I finish the story?

Ebony: No!

Darius: *(Darius smiles at the worried look on his sister's face.)* Let's tell jokes instead.

□   **I can read and comprehend grade-level fiction texts.**

Bear Scare

Use the play on page 86 to answer the questions.

1. At what time of day did this story occur? _____

   What are the clues? _____

   _____

2. Was Ebony afraid? _____

   How do you know? _____

   _____

3. Why did the author include the information in parenthesis? _____

   _____

   _____

4. Are you more like Ebony, Forrest, or Darius? Why? _____

   _____

   _____

   _____

   _____

☐ I can look back at a text to find answers.
☐ I can describe characters in a story.
☐ I can use proper terms to name parts of text.
☐ I can describe how the parts build upon each other.

Picnic Mystery

Read the story. Use context clues to infer the answers to the questions on page 89.

My friend Francine has a very vivid imagination. Her explanations for the most common events can be very colorful.

Last month, Francine's family and my family went on a picnic to the park. We played games, ran races, and eventually sat down to eat. First, we emptied my mom's picnic basket. She had packed hot dogs, buns, strawberry fruit bars (my favorite), and pretzels. Then, we began to empty the basket that Francine's mom had packed. Out came some egg salad sandwiches, potato salad, cold juice, and . . . !

"What happened to the potato chips?" exclaimed Mrs. Farmer. "There was a full bag of them when I packed the basket!"

"I bet I know what happened, Mom," Francine began to explain. "The ants at this park are **horrendous**! They must have chewed their way into the bag and carried away some of the chips!"

"You know how strong those little creatures are!" she continued, looking very serious. "I noticed some of them when Becky and I were climbing the hill. I'm sorry I didn't say something."

"That sounds a little **far-fetched**," replied Mrs. Farmer, "but maybe that could have happened. We'll discuss this matter further when we get home."

We sat down at the picnic table. I thought I heard some crunching noises when Francine plopped down on the bench. However, I may have been imagining it. Anyway, lunch was great—minus some of the chips!

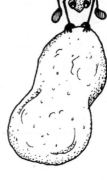

☐ **I can read and comprehend grade-level fiction texts.**

Picnic Mystery (cont.)

Use the story on page 88 to answer the questions.

1. Do you think Francine's explanation for the missing potato chips was accurate? _____

   Explain. _____

   _____

2. Did Mrs. Farmer totally accept Francine's explanation? _____

   How do you know?_____

3. Explain this statement: "Her explanations for the most common events can be very colorful."

   _____

   _____

4. Circle all of the words that best describe Francine's explanation for the missing potato chips.

   honest   sincere   mischievous   crafty

   imaginative   creative   kind   truthful

5. According to the text, what does *horrendous* mean?_____

   _____

6. According to the text, what does *far-fetched* mean? _____

   _____

7. What do you think really happened to the chips? _____

   _____

☐ **I can look back at the text to find answers.**
☐ **I can describe characters in a story.**
☐ **I can figure out the meaning of words and phrases in a story.**
☐ **I can compare my point of view to that of the narrator or characters.**

A Light in the Garden

Read the story. Answer the questions on page 91.

Hugo sat in the chair by the window. The grandfather clock by the stairs started to chime. It echoed through the quiet halls.

Hugo could hardly keep his eyes open. He knew his pajamas were laid out neatly on the bed, but he did not want to put them on. Tonight, he wanted to sleep in his clothes, not in the flannel pajamas with blue footballs all over them.

When his parents said he could stay with his uncle while they went to France, Hugo had been happy. His other choice was Camp Blue Sky. He hated Camp Blue Sky. At least at his uncle's house, he would have good food, a room of his own, and no camp crafts.

However, tonight Hugo was missing his parents.

Hugo closed his eyes and listened to the clock strike. He wished he had chosen Camp Blue Sky. At least there were other people around.

The clock stopped chiming. The huge house was very still. His uncle's bedroom was far down the hall. Hugo opened his eyes and looked out the window. He wanted to see something moving.

If he knew for sure somebody else was nearby, he might be able to sleep. Other people made him forget that Mom and Dad were far away.

At first, he saw nothing, just dark paths and the reflection of the moon in his uncle's pond. Then he saw it. At first, the white beam flickered. It became steady. It moved across the far side of the garden, just beyond the garage. When it came toward the house, Hugo no longer felt alone. But who was it? What was it?

He jumped in bed. He did not want anybody to see he had been missing his parents. His heart pounded. He heard the creaking boards. They sounded like footsteps. His bedroom door creaked open. Who could it be? Just then something soft and warm touched him. A wet tongue washed his face.

"Hugo, it's only me!" His uncle pulled a flashlight from his pocket and turned it on so he could see. "I brought Felix in out of the cold. He needs a place to sleep. Would it be OK for him to sleep in here? He always likes company."

Hugo laughed. "Yes. that would be great!"

I can read and comprehend grade-level fiction texts.

A Light in the Garden (cont.)

Use the story on page 90 to answer the questions.

1. Who is Felix? _____
   _____

2. Why did Hugo not want to go to bed? _____
   _____

3. What made the creaks that Hugo heard? _____
   _____
   _____

4. Why did Hugo's uncle come to Hugo's room? _____
   _____
   _____

5. How are you similar to Hugo? _____
   _____

6. How are you different from Hugo? _____
   _____

7. What kind of mood did the first half of the story create for the rest of the story?_____
   _____

8. Write a brief summary of this story.

   _____

   _____

   _____

   _____

☐   **I can retell stories using details and use them to understand the main idea.**
☐   **I can describe how the parts of a text build upon each other.**
☐   **I can compare my point of view to that of the narrator or characters.**

Answer Key

Page 12
1. a; 2. c; 3. a; 4. Answers will vary but may include greedy or proud. 5. It was easy for the fox to say he didn't want the grapes because he couldn't reach them. But, he really did want the grapes.

Page 13
1. S; 2. P; 3. P; 4. S; 5. P; 6. S

Page 15
1. Dylan; 2. Danny; 3. Dylan; 4. Dylan; 5. Danny; 6. Dylan; 7. Danny; 8. Danny; 9. Dylan; 10. Danny; 11. Dylan; 12. exciting, happy, interesting, good; 13. difficult, itchy, bad, tiring; 14. Answers will vary.

Page 17
1. c; 2. b; 3. c; 4. b; 5. c; 6. b; 7. tough, determined, scared; 8. caring, determined

Page 19
1. a; 2. c; 3. a; 4. c; 5. b

Page 21
1. Javier wanted a bike. 2. His family could not afford to buy a bike. 3. He offered to help Mrs. Martinez pull weeds in her garden because she could not do it alone. 4. Mrs. Martinez offered to give Javier her son's old bike in exchange

for helping her. 5. Answers will vary but may include: Both boys are caring towards others. Both boys had a positive experience. 6. Answers will vary but may include: Jorge wanted to take care of animals. Javier wanted a new bike.

Page 23
1. from Demitri's brother; 2. a watch; 3. by email; 4. They had just come from a field trip. 5. He did not want his mother to hear. 6. Sabena

Page 25
Web should be filled in as follows:

- Bitsy's food: acorns, nuts, bark, seeds, grass, mushrooms
- Bitsy's tree: oak tree
- The new guest: tall woman
- Bitsy's home: nest built of twigs, lined with soft fur and feathers
- The new guest's pet: Midnight, a black cat with leaf-green eyes
- The new pet's habit: sitting under the oak tree stalking Bitsy
- Bitsy might starve because she cannot get to the ground to eat.
- Bitsy was scared because the cat tried to attack her once before.

- Bitsy had to be careful of pets (cats and dogs), wild animals (foxes, raccoons, and hawks), Midnight.
- How Bitsy handled the problem: She got up early before the cat arrived. She jumped from branch to branch and climbed fences and rooftops to find safe places to eat.
- Time of year the problem stopped: autumn

Page 27
1. fifth; 2. second; 3. third; 4. first; 5. fourth; 6. before; 7. after; 8. before; 9. before; 10. before

Page 28
1. Ralph: his aunt's house; Sheila: her grandmother's house; 2. Ralph: too much work; Sheila: too little to do; 3. Answers will vary but may include: Ralph: tired; Sheila: bored; 4. Both characters mention going back to school soon.

Page 29
a. 5; b. 2; c. 1; d. 4; e. 3

Page 31
1. Cranebrook Heights, Mareville, playing soccer, park; 2. it was hot and the two neighborhoods were not getting along; 3. No one won. 4. They learned that they can get along.

Answer Key

Page 33

Check to see that students' crossed-out sentences are those with unnecessary information. 1. She thinks summer is boring. 2. She loves summer. 3. She realized it was almost over. 4. *Never* shows exaggeration. There are some fun times. 5. The correct order of sentences is 3, 1, 2, 5, 6, 4, 7.

Page 35

1. Answers will vary but may include: Cassie is a college student asked to do a babysitting job. She is confident, determined, and a hard worker. 2. Bettie is a young and mischievous child who causes trouble for Cassie. 3. a. She put her hand in the chocolate pudding. b. She threw spaghetti into the air. c. She tracked spaghetti through the house.

Page 37

1. Answers will vary but may include: a. She dumped the bubble bath into the tub. b. She kicked blocks all over the room. c. She threw spaghetti. 2. She became frustrated. She realized how much work it was to

babysit Bettie. 3. Answers will vary but may include: She didn't want to upset the parents. 4. Answers will vary but may include: It made it easier to remember everything Cassie had to do. 5. Answers will vary but may include: clean up after each activity, plan ahead, and bring board games to play.

Page 39

old, sell, look, truck, grandparents, yo-yo, broken, teddy bear, friend, keep, old; Answers will vary.

Page 41

1. This ad is trying to sell a toy called a Wuzzy Pet. 2. The ad says the toy feels warm and fuzzy, does tricks, makes animal noises, and you don't have to feed or bathe it. 3. The ad says the toy requires some assembly and that prices may vary. Also, batteries are not included with the toy. 4. Answers will vary. 5. The ad says not to spill liquid on it or place it in water. 6. Answers will vary but may include: They are selling Wuzzy Pets. They are warm and fuzzy, and do tricks. They make animal noises.

Page 43

1. Answers will vary but may include: He thinks it will be easy to take a class photo. He likes to say it because he is a photographer and they snap pictures. 2. The climax is when the class is outside and the wind keeps blowing and messing up the picture. a. 9; b. 10; c. 6; d. 5; e. 7; f. 2; g. 8; h. 1; i. 4; j. 3

Page 45

1. a; 2. An illness left Helen Keller blind and deaf when she was a baby. 3. A teacher named Annie Sullivan helped Helen Keller learn how to speak. 4. Answers will vary. 5. Answers will vary but may include: She did not hear and speak exactly like others, she probably had her own version of hearing and speaking. 6. The author thinks Helen Keller is a hard worker, very smart, and dedicated. Answers will vary.

Page 47

1. sequence, cause/effect; 2. They help seedlings grow and cause cones to release seeds. 3. The author thinks sequoias are the most amazing trees on Earth. Answers will vary. 4. Answers

Answer Key

will vary, but should include the words *forests*, *giant*, *sequoia*, *tall*, *million*, *warm*, and *fire*.

Page 48
a. hotel; b. with an uncle; c. having fun; d. bored and sick; e. Answers will vary but may include that she went to beach; f. Answers will vary but may include that she went shopping; g. shells; h. new book

Page 49
1. community garden; 2. retirement homes; 3. Antonio; 4. Annabelle; 5. Annabelle; 6. nature center guide; 7. piano

Page 51
1. different; 2. different; 3. same; 4. same; 5. morning; because it is cooler; 6. the Mojave Desert; 7. 60 years old; 8. It is hard for her to turn over again and she could die. 9. Answers will vary but may include: They showed what type of animal Sara was and what she looked like.

Page 53
1. b; 2. c; 3. It means freedom from outside control. 4. fireworks, flags, parades; 5. fireworks, concerts; 6. fireworks

Page 54
Check one item in each row. Answers will vary but should be either Hawaii or Solomon Islands.

Page 55
1. Answers will vary but should include three comparisons in sentence form. 2. Answers will vary but should include comparisons or contrasts regarding climate or weather in sentence form.

Page 56
Whales: salt, smooth, rubbery; up and down; blowhole; warm blooded, constant; Fish: fresh or salt; hard scales; side to side; gills; cold blooded, varies

Page 57
Marked with an X: 3, 6, 8; 9. a layer of fat; 10. a whale

Page 59
a. single, coiled; b. 2 shells, hinged together; c. eight shell plates; d. North America; e. both North American coasts; f. Pacific Ocean; g. limpets, slugs, snails; h. clams, oysters, muscles, scallops; i. bounded and mossy mopalia; 4. Answers will vary but may include: They showed what each type of mollusk looks like. They helped to better

explain the description in the text.

Page 60
Students should draw add webbed feet, a bill, and a flat tail.

Page 61
Diagram labels: bill, webbed feet, tail; 1. a; 2. a; 3. b; 4. c; 5. a; 6. d; 7. b

Page 63
1. T; 2. F; 3. T; 4. T; 5. F; 6. F; 7. F; 8. T; 9. comparison; 10. Answers will vary.

Page 64
1. Answers will vary but may include: She was unsure of her artistic abilities. She was proud of her artwork; 2. Answers will vary but may include: He remembered all of his old friends and really liked the painting.

Page 66
1. Chapter 1 explains that Jana is afraid to speak in front of others. 2. She became more confident in her speaking abilities. 3. she wanted the prize money to help her family. 4. they wanted to tell their family they won. 5. Answers will vary but may include: They both are girls and they are in the same science fair. 6. Jana is afraid to speak in

Answer Key

front of others, and Yolanda is not. Yolanda works well with electronics and Jana does not. 7. Answers will vary but may include: It created a problem for the girls. 8. Answers will vary but may include: Take deep breaths or pretend you are talking to a friend.

Page 67
1. Answers will vary but may include: They are thrill-seeking, fun-loving people.
2. There is no gravity.
3. high fuel prices;
4. Answers will vary but may include: Someone might not like this trip if they are afraid of flying.

Page 68
Answers will vary but may include: 1. so scientists could share information; 2. It described how information was passed. 3. It was hard to share information with scientists in different countries without the World Wide Web.

Page 70
1. he thought it would be boring. 2. there was a party. 3. it was loud and exciting. 4. he had never danced when people were watching. 5. his sister told him he was a good dancer. 6. Yes, his heart jumped

from excitement. 7. Answers will vary but may include: In the beginning, Allen felt upset. In the end, Allen was having fun and was excited.

Page 71
Answers will vary but may include: 1. the dancers fly through the air. 2. she wants to be a ballerina. 3. she thinks it will make her a ballerina. 4. she was afraid she was not going to be a ballerina. 5. she is going to school to become a ballerina.

Page 72
1. a huge wave;
2. earthquakes; 3. damage;
4. they want to save lives.
5. it can warn people when tsunamis are coming and they can seek safety.
6. Answers will vary but may include: It is about earthquakes and how much damage they can cause. It is about tsunamis and how big they can be. It is also about how scientists are trying to make people safer.

Page 73
1. 1; 2. An aurora borealis is one of the brightest night-time lights. It is like light dancing across the sky. 3. 2; 4. charged particles, solar flares; 5. hydrogen; 6. powdered metal

Page 74
Answers will vary but may include: 1. An aurora borealis is a bright light. 2. a. It is caused by particles that reflect light. b. It is also cause by eruptions of gas on the sun. 3. The Hindenburg mysteriously exploded in 1937. 4. a. People thought hydrogen gas had caused the explosion. b. Now people think it may have been a powdered metal that caused it to explode. 5. "Lights in the Sky:" aurora borealis, bright lights, nighttime, reflection of light, solar flares; Both: happen in the sky, mysterious; "Explosion in the Sky:" Hindenburg, caused by chemicals, hydrogen gas

Page 76
1. c; 2. c; 3. a; 4. b; 5. Answers will vary but may include: They help you see what the text is describing.

Page 77
Answers will vary but may include: 1. erosion; 2. The bottom is softer and erodes faster. 3. They want to slow erosion. 4. Niagara Falls will keep eroding because you cannot stop water and therefore the erosion.

Answer Key

Page 78
1. c; 2. b; 3. b; 4. Answers will vary but may include: They help you see what the kids are building as well as their emotions.

Page 79
1. Mars; because the planet is red and the aliens are Martians; 2. Saturn; The astronaut asks how close they are to Saturn.

Page 80
1. Texas, New York; 2. cat, He wags his tail, curls into a ball, and meows. 3. rabbit, She has soft fur, long ears, a bushy tail, and hops.

Page 81
1. b; 2. not in order; 3. b; 4. Answers will vary. 5. Answers will vary but may include: "Tests of Building Materials" and "The Three Little Pigs" have the same characters. "Tests of Building Materials" is told from the wolf's point of view, and "The Three Little Pigs" is told from the narrator or pig's point of view.

Page 83
1. baseball. He wore a mitt and was a pitcher. 2. a; 3. nervous. His stomach twisted. 4. confident; He smiled. 5. simile; 6. The tigers were giants. 7. to make a mean face; 8. Whump!, Swish!

Page 85
Answers will vary but may include: 1. This report will impress you. 2. Similar: A character named Jack grows a beanstalk. Different: Jack does not admit to using magic beans in this article. 3. a, d; The airports are closed. 4. b, c; They touch the sky and are very large. They need support poles.

Page 87
1. at night, They need a fire to see. 2. Yes. She was shaking. 3. to show what action the character is making; 4. Answers will vary.

Page 89
Answers will vary but may include: 1. No. It seems unbelievable. 2. No. She said it sounded far-fetched. 3. It means she makes up wild stories. 4. mischievous, crafty, imaginative, creative; 5. terrible; 6. unbelievable, unlikely; 7. Answers will vary but may include: Francine ate them.

Page 91
1. a dog; 2. He was missing his parents. 3. his uncle coming to his room; 4. His uncle came to help Hugo not feel lonely by bringing the dog in. 5. Answers will vary. 6. Answers will vary. 7. a sad mood; 8. Answers will vary but may include: Hugo was staying at his uncle's house and was feeling lonely. Then, Hugo's uncle brought his dog inside to keep Hugo company.

© Carson-Dellosa • CD-104660